Cougarman Percy Dewar

Liza Potvin

Order this book online at www.trafford.com
or email orders@trafford.com

Most Trafford titles are also available at major online book retailers.

Print information available on the last page.

ISBN: 978-1-4120-5877-3 (sc)
ISBN: 978-1-4122-3622-5 (e)

Trafford rev. 02/13/2023

Trafford
PUBLISHING® www.trafford.com
North America & international
toll-free: 844-688-6899 (USA & Canada)
fax: 812 355 4082

Cougarman Percy Dewar

THE SUN is just setting on the canyon and its long rays touch with a rosy luminescence the great upthrust tumbled rocks where ridge and spur meet, bringing to them the look of a large medieval castle in ruins, glowing from a fire that consumes it. Far in the distance to the east the high point of the ridge, beneath which the cougar's ledge lies, is also touched by rosy light, but all else is in shadow. Nothing moves beneath his view but several nighthawks working the slope below, hopping erratically and momentarily catching the light and them vanishing below the shadow line. Beneath the spur's slope below the cougar is a flat, parklike meadow, lined with trees. He yawns, rolls to his feet, and stretches with his hindquarters high and his forelegs extended before him; his curved claws, from which few prey animals ever pulled free, scrape on the rock and are retracted. He straightens with the grace that is inherent in all his movements, rubs his chin with pleasure on a protruding stone, and walks to the front of the canyon ledge on big, padded feet, surveying the canyon below. Sitting there, he resembles a great, strongly-muscled domestic cat but has a proportionately smaller head, smaller, rounded ears, white lips, and a pale belly. Then slowly he stretches again and begins moving along the ledge. In the gathering darkness, he moves toward the open meadow. As he approaches, he sets his course to make a swing around it and approach from the downhill side to get the descending breeze. The cougar's broad head is thrust forward and swings a little with the steady gait of his walk. His yellow eyes are half-closed. His huge shoulders work smoothly, making his stride appear shorter than it actually is. The cougar's body is supple and graceful, and the slight suggestion of clumsiness in the long hind legs is offset by the majestic flow of his long tail, held straight down nearly to the ground, where the tip of it is caught up and held in a sharp little curve. His colours blend almost perfectly with any degree of light or shade. A black line along his back, the mark that seems peculiar to the cougars of the northern part of Vancouver Island, shades through dark brown to tawny lion colour on his sides, shoulders, and haunches, while his belly and chest are lighter still. He is rugged, powerful, and sinister. Magnificent.

The cougar paces steadily and silently at the top of a ridge half way down the canyon, having scented the buck below. The smell is faint but intermittent. His pace slows, but he does not crouch low yet. With darkness for a cover, he can afford a high head. He stops and moves upwind to better catch the scent, then waits for sound, making no noise himself. There is a slight crackling of twigs below. The pupils of his eyes expand to a fierce glare, then contract. The tip of his tail twitches back and forth. That is all. There is no other warning, no sign of ferocity or eagerness, no indication of muscles keyed to the pitch of flawless action. With three great, smooth bounds, the cougar leaps on the deer's back, and the deer's head snaps around. Looking backwards. The cougar hooks one big front paw into the buck's nose and opens its mouth to bite into the deer's neck. Almost a kiss. The cougar's near front leg is held down over the deer's back, holding onto the shoulder. Making not a sound. Taking hardly any time. The deer makes no attempt to run nor does he struggle to get free. The cougar and the deer simply twist and writhe together in a slow dance, settling slowly toward the ground. The buck cries out once and then dies. Death is simple, fascinating. A mystery.

Here is another mystery: all the native totem poles on the West Coast honour many animals, but not all include the Cougar. The Nootka actively disliked the mountain lion and claimed not to have understood its nature. There are few extant myths or stories about the cougar. The only myth I've read involves the cougar's disreputable performance as the malevolent animal that clawed the whale's body from chin to breastbone, which is how the whale came to have slits alongside its body. Yet every Native culture except those in the Arctic encountered the cougar, attested to by the many names by which it became known to European settlers.

Has the cougar always inspired awe and reverence? Or just fear? Or is its existence so shadowy and invisible that it might be inviting a wrathful encounter with the spirit world to depict the Cougar at all? Some think the cougar so mysterious and sneaky that they wonder if it is real; only the morning evidence of its carnage confirms its existence. Only big eyes glowing in the dark. A half-glimpsed shadow seen between the trees. Possibly the source of evil. How to depict something never seen very clearly? And who would dare to take on the mask of the Cougar? How to search for his spirit when his presence is sensed out there but never verified by the light of day?

These and other mysteries have long haunted one man who has spent his whole life on Vancouver Island and knows it intimately: Percy Dewar. His life story is a fascinating one: he spent the first half of it hunting cougars, and the second half, attempting to preserve them. My life is remarkably different from his, but somehow we sense in one another a kindred spirit. Over the years, Percy has become part of my family. But I must back up, and mention how we met:

Once upon a time, my marriage fell apart. I did not know who I was. What corner of the world do we choose to search for answers? Or does it choose us? I went to Strathcona Park and got into a canoe on Buttle Lake for a solo canoe trip so that I could clear my mind. It was a time when I was seeking to build up my confidence again. At the lodge, I registered for a rope-climbing course, determined to overcome my fear of heights. One day on my canoe trip, I met a strange man who had Akbash hounds – a breed of dog I had never met before. I did not want to trespass on his property, as he clearly wished to be undisturbed. He was spry, under 5'10", with an iron grey crew-cut, unassuming in appearance.

He seemed bashful but somehow dangerous, aloof. Days later, eating lunch at the Strathcona Park Lodge, there was the man again, being fed by the lodge owner in return for chores he had completed. The owner, Merna Bolding, claims that Percy has lifetime dining privileges at the lodge, after all the work he has done from them. When I asked what his "chores" consisted of, Percy described his most recent job for the lodge. At sixty-nine years old, Percy was putting in sixty hydro poles around Strathcona Park. Here is what he told me of that project:

"The Lodge decided to put in a hydro plant. This involved a pelting wheel at the lake and a pipeline a mile up the mountain and a damn in the creek that is three miles away from the lodge. So it's taken sixty poles to carry the power to the lodge itself. There are some old logging roads already on the mountain, so I decided to work on them and repair them since there had been a lot of slides. It took a huge amount of work to make them driveable. I used my bulldozer on the roads, and also to drag the poles to where they had to go. The holes had to be dug, of course, so it's taken me most of a year to get that much done. There were six young guys working on the job, and once the poles were in, they had to climb. I went up all the poles but two!"

I asked him what else he did by way of maintenance around the lodge. He told me that he got the pipeline started up each spring time and maintained it throughout the winter. He once spent several weeks realigning the pipes to improve the flow. And he told me the story of how his dog Magee, observing Percy carrying the 330 ft. plastic pipes, began to carry them to aid his master.

Magee helps build pipeline

"I've never stopped being amazed at how smart dogs are, smarter than human beings in many ways. That dog Magee has always served me well. Actually, I call him Gee. I try to give all my dogs simple names so that it is easier for them to remember. And easier to call them all in a hurry! The dog Molly I had around the same time as Magee, she knew over five hundred words, I'm certain of it. I used to test her all the time. Supposedly dogs can't distinguish colours, but eventually Molly knew to fetch me my red handknitted socks when I asked for them, and not to bring me the green ones."

"One time I hired this pilot to take me out to Creycroft Island because I was considering doing a study there; we took a Beaver from Campbell River to get there, and his price was seventy-two cents a mile. I paid for the return trip in advance, and he was supposed to pick me up after five days. But he never showed up. So I hailed a fishing boat to radio that pilot after waiting out in the woods for an extra day. When he got out to let me outta the plane, my dog peed all over him and I never did apologize. I swear my dog knew that I'd been insulted and wasn't going to put up with any insults."

"Another time, I learned that dogs can feel insulted themselves. I usually find deer that cougar have killed by letting the slower dog that I used for trailing find the deer, since I could always hear her when the others ran ahead. If there is a cougar in the area, you know for sure there is a kill nearby. I could see where the cougar had come out the trail, and wanted her to trace its tracks by going backwards, but she did not want to do it because she knew it was the wrong way. Instead she walked home by herself, a whole ten miles, because she would rather do that than backtrack. She knew the difference and felt insulted. Now I know that dogs have personalities after that incident."

"I got letters from people in Alberta and other places where I sold my pups to, and they were full of praise for those dogs, agreeing that there were everything I said they would be. Even into their old age, those hounds stood me well. I had three ten-year-old hounds when I started my study, and everyone thought they wouldn't make it, but they all lived for a dozen years after that. I certainly have been blessed with good dogs all my life."

Percy never minces words, has a light sense of humour, a twinkle in his eye, and has a philosophical twist to all his tales, in spite of the fact that he is a man who prefers physical labour to reflection. We talked. He discovered that I was a writer. At the end of our talk, which lasted only a couple of hours but seemed much longer, he asked me to write his life story. It seemed a strange request from someone who was a relative stranger, but in talking with Percy I felt a deep connection, as if we had known one another for a lifetime. I began visiting him in Strathcona whenever I could get away from work, and started recording his story on a tape recorder and in my notes.

"I was born on Vancouver Island and grew up at a time when there were more animals than people here. My knowledge of wildlife was passed on to me by my father, and I have learned a lot since," he says. "In the twenties, I used to go walking with my dad along the logging railway in the evening, and it was possible to count up to 80 deer in an hour, and just as many blue grouse. It stayed that way until the early fifties. With the high deer population, the predators increased; bears, cougars, and wolves thrived on all the berries too."

I was afraid to embark on this voyage. Taking stock of a life. Writing about my own life seemed acceptable, but it was presumptuous to try to describe the significant moments in someone else's life. That was a decade ago. I have since made many trips into the bush, and later to Salt Spring Island, where Percy now makes his home, to meet with the man. He still remains an enigma. He gives me a shoebox with all his photographs in it – a lifetime contained in a box. In spite of his reluctance to divulge facts about himself, and in spite of his having a personality that does not lean toward the speculative or the introspective, I continue to ponder the mystery of his life.

And I am learning from Percy. How to walk in the dark woods, mostly. How to follow the cougar, as we all must. How prey controls the numbers of cougars, not the other way around. How history is full of cruelty, sensationalism, poisonings, maimings, torture, sin. How you can begin with biology, or politics, or you can begin with family and loyalty, but you end up in the same place: one group devouring another. How I need to respect my elders, who may offer us the only way out of this predatory pattern.

Percy is older and wiser than me, his generation a dying breed of Renaissance men and women, pioneers who know how to clear land, build houses, grow gardens, preserve their own food, build and repair anything needed around a household. People who knew how to entertain themselves before the arrival of television, videos, and computers. People who had little money, but seemed to lead richer, happier lives than we do today.

I am exactly half his age. He is closer to death than I am, so there is a certain urgency in telling his story. He tells me how much he has learned from cougars, especially how to live his life leisurely. How to stop along the "bench" edges of a bluff and take in the long view. Cougars stop while being tracked to mark a tree, almost as if to say, "I'm safe. You can't get me."

Here are a few facts he has gleaned through years of personal observation of cougars, facts he tells me are necessary if I intend to spend any time at all in the bush:

"A cougar doesn't usually waste meat, except in times of over-plenty; he will often gorge himself on the kill and then starve for days. Meat-eating birds do gather at deer kills or other kills. And sometimes ravens feed where a cougar has killed, so a good hunter can tell from the note of their calls where the cougar is feeding. You can tell the difference between a cougar kill and a wolf kill by the untidiness of the wolf kill."

Percy explains that wolves tear meat from bone and bone from bone, scattering the debris in all directions; they hunt in packs, so they finish the kill in a single meal and so don't need that instinct not to waste meat since there will be none left over. The cougar plucks bunches of hair from the hide over the short ribs, and works with the short teeth in the front of his upper and lower jaws so that the hide can be exposed to the long sharp tusks he has in each side of his jaws. "I once heard that it's a good thing that he swallows some of those hairs, because they line the stomach to keep it clear of tapeworms and the like. He doesn't usually expose the guts when he kills the deer, just eats the ribs first. But when he starts chewing on the ribs like that, the guts drop out to the ground and all the gases go into the air, instead of bloating the carcass within a few hours."

"A cougar will not touch tainted meat. Unless it is really sick or really old or something. When the cougar is done with his prey, usually deer, the stomach, hide, and lower leg bones are left behind. He covers the stomach with leaves or whatever else is near. In our study, we found that the female cougar is very fussy about her meat. She slits the game open, then rolls the stomach and guts to one side. She'll clip away the hairs with her teeth, then, when she's had her fill, she'll wrap up the rest in the skin like a bedroll to protect it from others eating it, and put it under a bush."

"Deer act nervous when a cougar is nearby, yet at times I have seen them go on eating even when the cougar was very near. The scent on cougar markings is similar to the spray from a house cat. If you watch a cougar clean himself, he licks his fur clean very slowly and washes his face with the inside of his wrist – you know, just like a cat, even rubbing his back against the rocks, then sitting and curling his tail around his feet. And you know, they even sound like regular cats when they holler, only louder and with a deeper growl at times. They keep in touch with each other by long, shrill calls that start at low volume, then get raised up, and drop low again as they end. Cougars vocalize at mating time, and I have also heard them scream when they are fighting hounds or being cornered by hounds."

"I have watched them do their mating dance: they kinda stare at one another at first like it's a showdown. Then the male will start flicking the tip of his tail and give a low moan, and the female won't let him get too close to her at first. She isn't used to his aggression, and will get sorta playful and tease him before letting him get real close. She'll sometimes walk ahead of him and stop and look back at him to see if he's following. Then she might lie down and roll around as if she's inviting him. But if he gets too aggressive all at once, she will move off and yowl at him and lay back her ears, and he'll start yowling back. It is quite the racket. Not the sort of scene many people get to see. I've been really lucky that way."

"Cougars will use trails that people have made or that people use a lot, and they will be on these trails or to the side of them where there is broken-down wood or any soft material – where they leave what are called scratch marks, on which they spray their scent. These scratch marks are six to eight inches wide and eight to twelve inches long."

I read about a cougar attack in the local newspaper and can't decide if I am fascinated or horrified. The eyes that stare back at me in the mirror some mornings do not seem to belong to me. When I talk to Percy, when he enters the realm of memory and tells me his stories, I am often confused about where the animal world begins and the human takes over. As if he were wearing a mask. Eyes glazed, he is transported into the world of storytelling. His gaze is as aloof as that of a cat. He is as agile as a mountain lion, lean and sinewy. Almost as shy. After I have visited for a day or two, he makes it clear that it is time for me to leave, time for him to be alone. He can tolerate human company only so long. This reminds me that there is something savagely masculine under the shy mystery of the feline grace of a cougar. Both are creatures of the shadows.

He gives me more facts about cougars. One of the few true carnivores left, cougars do not procure their meat through family cooperation, as wolves do. Except for mothers with young, lions live and hunt alone. The mother doesn't usually roam far from them until two or three weeks after the cubs' eyes are opened, and then she nearly always travels at night. And when she returns to them from feeding, she circles and doubles and waits on her tracks to make certain that she is not followed. Her tremendously powerful muscles and tendons and sinews need to be working efficiently in order to ensure her own survival. Soon the urge to roam becomes stronger than her urge to be with her cubs. Yet her thoughts are never far from them, and although she roams in vague, irregular circles, she could always go back to them by the straightest of straight lines if a sudden intuitive anxiety drives her back. If the mother is killed while the cubs are young, is there some species memory that is lost or interrupted? Percy doesn't know.

Percy also lives and hunts alone, like a cougar. Or until he becomes so ill that he can no longer look after himself. He likes to stick fairly close to his home range, and is rarely seen, like a cougar. He rarely goes to the city, and has never had the desire to leave Vancouver Island. Like a cougar, he learned most of what he has learned through trial and error. "Get your basic skills first in life, then strengthen and hone them until you are ready to assert them," he tells me. "This goes for hunting as it does for anything else in life. There's a time for using your power and skills forcefully, like a cougar striking without hesitation. When you feel threatened, you go for the vulnerable spot – I learned that too. Just like a cougar is the only animal that can kill a porcupine without harming himself, by flipping it onto its back and exposing the underbelly. And then there's other times when you want to assert power more gently -- like the cougar's main prey, the deer. It seems to me I have learned a lot from watching both the hunter and the hunted most of my life. I am not afraid of using my power, and sometimes this can offend other people, but I'm well past caring what others think about me. I'm the kind of person who seems to attract a lot of attention when I do something or make a statement, and I fall under attack quite easily."

Here is a fact: he has never worn a watch in his life. "We shouldn't be controlled by time. I like to wake up when the sun comes up, and get to bed shortly after it gets dark. It's how I've lived my whole life, and it seems the most natural."

Another fact: Percy's organs are reversed. He's literally all backwards. Percy tells me that a doctor came to visit his school in Extension one year to vaccinate the children. Percy was instructed to bend over, touch his toes ten times, and then have the doctor listen to his heart. The doctor could not locate Percy's heartbeat, so he was sent to Ladysmith for x-rays, and there he discovered that his heart, his stomach, and his liver were all located on the reverse side of his body. The opposite of normal. Did he feel that this marked him, set him apart? Percy laughs, and readily admits that, while he did not think this discovery an omen, he has always known that he was different from most people, and suggests that

that might account for his desire to live apart. "Knew I was backwards from the beginning!" he jokes.

I often wonder whether I haven't got things backwards too. I wonder if I have lost my better half, or found my better half here in the bush. What does it mean to have your heart on the wrong side? To be divided down the centre? To be half man, half animal? If you are built differently, do you think differently, feel differently?

But it is not just his body that is mysterious and camaflouged. Not just his heart that does not beat in an expected place. He wears a mask too. I do not know if the mask is worn to inspire fear, or to isolate himself from others. To be the stalker.

Masks create barriers. Masks create security, refuge. Men become animals behind masks, become multiple selves, identify with cosmic forces. The wearer of the mask not only represents the spirit of the mask, he becomes – he is – this spirit. He makes something that has disappeared reappear again. Human individuality is lifted from him. He is transformed. He is not himself.

Percy says that when he looks in the mirror, he is often taken aback – usually because it has been so long since he last looked at himself that he does not recognize the man in the mirror. He says that if he didn't have a mirror, and look in it occasionally, he might disappear entirely, lose any sense of who he is, become invisible to himself.

Cougars are also often invisible. Even if there are no totemic figures of cougars, their presence on Vancouver Island is palpable. Human confrontation with the wild sometimes takes on mythic proportions, as when, in 1989 in Oak Bay, a suburb of Victoria, a woman in a basement apartment found herself staring at a cougar on the other side of her street level window. Denise Mueller was in her bedroom applying makeup when a wild mountain lion came crashing through the window. Either it believed it saw another cougar in its reflection, or the basement suite reminded it of a cave. "I froze in terror. I looked into the monstrous, snarling cat's jaws and I was sure I was going to die," said Denise. But what is it she really encountered in the glass? Perhaps, like the cougar, she saw her own fearful reflection too. Perhaps we all need mirrors to know ourselves.

Percy sees cougars for what they are. "People look at a cougar and just see their own fear. They expect service from Fish and Wildlife in getting rid of cougars when they feel threatened by them, but refuse to protect themselves against predators by keeping decent and large-sized dogs when they are in the bush. The Saanich Penninsula is still wild, and there are lots of deer. People get annoyed that deer eat their gardens, but want to shoot the cougars that would keep the deer population down. Cougars will always come there in search of deer. Who is going to fire the first shot? What is the law of the land, and who will make the first break in the food chain? Who is going to outlive whom?"

I have always known that I am part animal and that I crave wide stretches of space. That I would be willing to fight to preserve that space. That I too might be divided down the middle, part civilized and part wild. When Percy says that he could happily spend all his life in the bush, that he is more comfortable with animals, whom he considers more rational than most human beings, I understand him.

Percy has tracked cougars for most of his eighty years. "You see, the problem is with our encroaching on their territory. There is no 'cougar problem', never has been. But there is a big human problem." He returns to the topic of their famed invisibility. Percy maintains that there are no native myths about cougars because First Nations people held the cougar in awe; some native guides he worked with told him that fear of and respect for the cougar prevented many from even uttering its name, which they considered sacred. There are no cougars in the Queen Charlottes, where Percy has guided; nor are they in the extreme north. Cougars hunt from dusk to dawn only, unless they have been unsuccessful the night before. Seldom seen, they are silent except for cries of rage or love. Is it just their invisibility that lends them mystery. Was the cougar once a deity? The Kwakiutl myth claims that the deer was originally a man but was transformed, on account of his intention to kill the son of a deity, into his present shape.

Unlike the pioneers of Percy's generation, who could work in the coal mines, hunt, log, fish, build, and farm, I have become overspecialized in my work and know far less about the world than my grandfather did. Time is stalking me now. Wouldn't we all secretly like to abandon mortgage and car payments, throw out the television, and head to the woods? In my next life, I plan to be more resourceful and self-reliant. Not living on the edge. So I ask Percy for advice. Here is what he tells me.

LOOK TALL. It is one way to see the world. This is the most important thing that Percy has shown me. Take charge, take control without hesitating. I am always tracing his footsteps. He has taught me how to move in the woods stealthily, attentively. He has taught me how to walk, all over again. To notice where the black bear bites the bark of a hemlock in spring, so a measure can be taken of its new height since the last spring. To know when a cougar is over two years old, when the black bars on its ears begin to diminish. Likewise the spot marks on the insides of the legs disappear at two years, melting into a fawn colour. "That's how I know, when I see on t.v. these markings on the 'murdering cougars' they show being captured and killed, that they are just young, ignorant animals whose mother has been taken from them before they were properly trained."

I walk in the woods with Percy and he tells me things I am eager to know. He teaches me never to walk in puddles, because that is where animals often leave their prints. "If you notice cougar prints in mud puddles, you can be sure they are within ten square miles. That is one thing I learned in my study of them. And another thing. Biologists say that cougars hate getting wet, but I've seen them swim rivers easily if they are being chased. And while it is common wisdom that cougars eat only at night, that's true only when humans are around. Mostly they don't seem to care if it is dark or light, and move and hunt whenever they get the urge." Percy's shoulders are squared back when he tells me this. He moves with an agile strength. I've watched him scale a tree with more ease than most thirty-year olds, and he is proud of it.

NEVER TAKE YOUR EYES OFF IT. "Look at a cougar straight on. Slow down. Do not submit, just back away. If a cougar has a big head, it is generally a male. Do not come between a female and her kittens. Give cougars an exit. After all, they are being crowded out, in spite of their ability to adapt well." He is surprised by the increase in the number of abnormal cougar behaviour reports. "Most of them are just adolescents, separated from their mothers before they have had time to learn how to hunt properly. Of course they'll attack anything small, they're hungry and we have deprived them of their prey."

NEVER APPROACH A COUGAR. "Just a while ago, in a logging area, a cougar killed a deer, and I could hear bones being chewed. That never would have happened before. Cougars are now accustomed to loud noise and activity of humans nearby. And I never heard of a standing adult being attacked. That attack near Lytton, that was a kid crawling out of a culvert. Somebody should have taught that kid never to crawl in the woods. And no one should ever disturb food caches, which you can sight by the soil and leaf litter the cougar covers the kill with. Just walk around it. If I came along and messed up the dinner you had carefully prepared, that would give you good reason to attack me, wouldn't it? But if you left what was mine alone, I wouldn't bother you."

DO NOT RUN. "Look tall. Do all you can to enlarge your size. When you meet a cougar, you must come into your own power and challenge the cougar. You would never let your kids out onto the street without teaching them the difference between a red and a green light. Well, you should also teach them never go out into the woods without a walking stick. Use a walking stick in the woods, and put your shirt or jacket or sweater on it and wave it above your head. Cougars can't see too good, and will mistake you for a very large animal. Let them know who is boss. Do not turn your back on a cougar. Remain upright. Down on all fours, you are vulnerable."

STAY CALM. Talk to the cougar in a confident voice.

Percy says he believes it when Natives tell him that in the beginning, there were only animals on the earth. It makes me want to return. To the time before our present time. When people were animals, and animals became human at will, and we all spoke the same language. When hunting meant killing relatives. And the hunter howled to the coyotes, identified with the predator, and offered a share of his kill to the coyotes. Sharing food with the largest family. Not buying individual, cellophane-wrapped portions of meat from my grocery store freezer. Not pacing back and forth in my urban cage.

I am Cougar. I will tell my story. It is different from those stories
told about me. All I ever wanted from the earth was to wander
it freely. At first I was the land itself. I crouched down on my
haunches to capture what was mine by right. When I turned on
my side, I was the hill under freezing stars. I did not need to see. I
was seen by all. It is true that my vision is not as good as yours. Yet

you can still never really see me. I am a nebulous creature, skirting the light at the edge of the shadowy forests of Vancouver Island. I am the master of all predators, who submit to me. I am the master of the Edge: most active at the brink of night and day, and I seek game on the prey-rich margins where one habitat abuts another. I am chestnut brown, less yellow than my tawny cousin on the mainland. Silent, alert, I stalk without distraction, eyes fixed upon the horizon. Like you humans, I need space. And space and time are running out. You have made us nearly extinct in Eastern Canada. So who is the more humane of the two kinds of creatures? I end up on trails I have always used but now there are people there. I will follow you, move with you and follow your crops that bring me my beloved deer. When I sight my prey, I crouch like one of your house cats, my tail twitching. Say a man grew up with hounds, training them to track us for years, went into the wilderness, spent many days on the trails. Does he believe he has earned the privilege of shooting us? The chase I understand. Perhaps there is some biological basis for your hunting urge. But why shoot a lion every year again and again? How can you make a living from the forest by shooting its denizens?

Once we too lived a simpler life. It was pleasant to lie on a rock in the full warmth of the sun. Pleasant to curl up in the dry shelter of a root in a night of storm and heavy, cold rain. Pleasant to swim across a river to get somewhere. The taste of fresh steaming meat, the crunching of bone against teeth, is the best pleasure of all -- to feed a hunger. The joy of power in smooth muscles stretched to their fullest, the satisfaction of the full stroke of a forepaw. These are the natural rhythms of our lives. You would understand if you too lived in harmony with nature, with the purpose of your lives.

At first some of us lived our whole lives out on Vancouver Island without becoming aware of the existence of man. We never wandered down to the beaches for food until we were driven to do so. At first there was no good prey, no beautiful Black-Tail Deer, in the old growth forests, so we were scarce before Contact, left the native settlements alone along the coast. Several hundred years ago, you actually thought I was a leopard because I have spots when I am young, but the spots disappear as I mature. So I do not stand out. Instead I wear the grasses around me like a matching variegated veil. You do know my mask. You know me by the name Tsonoqua, and the natives called me Wild Woman of the Woods. Have you heard my scream when I am in estrus? How many times you have had to justify your fear of my scream by eradicating its source, killing your own unacceptable weakness! And so we began to grow hungry. How long will you continue to persecute my kind? We can go no further west without dropping off into the ocean. You used to poison our meat. You bragged about how many of us you could "bag" in a week. And it is always me, the female with small kittens, who is more likely to be shot than the male, simply because I leave a more visible network of tracks as I hunt for my young!

Now that you have logged these woods, I can get to your settlements more easily. I come down into your towns beside the new highway, watch the deer in your newly planted vegetation. As you succeed further as a species, I recede further from your reach. Invisible, mysterious, sly and secretive, I am a solitary creature whose presence you can sense from the way the hairs on the back of you neck stand up. You wonder if you are being stalked. I am crouched along a sloping log, motionless, inconspicuous, watching. Above you on this lonely ridge, I have watched you long enough, observed you patiently, indulged your limitations. Your arrogance is astounding. Your belief that this land is yours, that gazing at it could absorb you eternally. I am prepared to force clarity upon you. I will show you what you truly desire -- not belief, but submission to a final authority. This depends upon violence. I have all the power of the night behind me. That is why the Midewiwim call me the Dream-Bringer. I am Cat as Sleep. I approach you silently, while you are dreaming, so you are never certain if you have really seen me or not.

I know nothing. Only empty space ahead of me, confusion behind. I want to be able to follow my nose. Percy tells me to keep walking.

Cougars usually live about 12 years, he claims. Percy says he can't smell cougars. Sometimes they spray, and the scent resembles house cat spray. Their cries sound like cat fights. He is adamant that they are not territorial, that the males leave their scratchings in the soil, covered in scent, only so that the female will be enticed to follow, not to mark out territory, as most researchers have claimed. Later I will read books by biologists who insist that cougars are territorial, especially the female. Some will claim that it is the female who leaves these markings for the male. Percy tells me to stop reading so much and spend more time observing in the bush. "Don't believe everything you read," he tells me. He claims that most of these books also do not see that the cougar is simply there, that any explanation of its mystery can therefore only be an excess. Percy believes that most of the writers who describe cougars are armchair adventurers who like to sensationalize violence in the natural world. "None of them have actually spent as long as I have with cougars," he insists. All of the descriptions of cougars do seem contaminated with longing and fear. But I believe Percy's descriptions. He has watched longer than most people. Percy holds me back and then shows me the scratch marks in the dirt, tells me that these ones are recent. On his hands and knees, he demonstrates how these scratches are made in the soil, how they indicate direction. Down on all fours, he looks vulnerable again, diminished.

Percy says that cougars switch their tails when they are annoyed, anxious, or catching prey. That when you watch them carefully, they do it too, as if they are curious or puzzled. That their tongues are rough enough to scrape meat off a hide. I think of the kiss of death. Cougars do a lot of things that domestic cats do. Later Percy shows me a picture of a cougar stretched against a hemlock like a huge domestic tabby working against a scratching post. It looks both tame and savage.

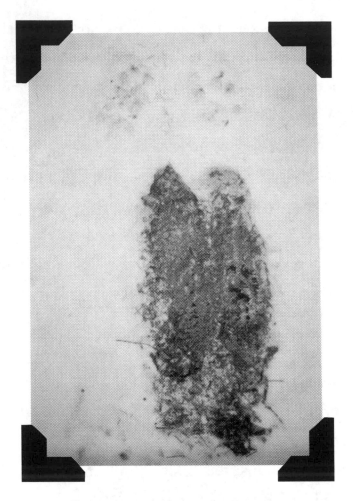

Cougar scratch marks in snow

    The scratch marks are not territorial, he insists. They are made by the male cougar balancing on his front feet and pushing back the soft matter with his hind feet simultaneously. Then the females, when they are in season, can pick up the scent and follow the males. When cougars are on a trail they will make these markings whenever they come near suitably soft material. If the cougar is turning off the trail, he will make a marking that faces in the direction he is heading. "Don't try this, men!" warns Percy. "It only works for cougars. The cougar will use the same path over and over. To be a success at hunting cougar, you must be as consistent as the cougar is, and your hounds must be just as consistent."

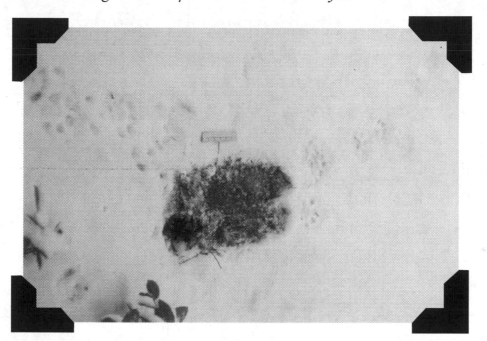

Cougar track in snow

Percy thinks that cougars were not native to the island, but have been driven further and further west as the mainland became more developed. "I hear all kinds of people who don't know what they are talking about claim to know the number of cougars here. But after my 1978 study, I would guess that there are only about 400 cougars left on the island." The domestic collides with the wild, until there is no place further west to which cougars can be pushed, without falling off the edge of the continent itself.

The wild and the civilized keep overlapping all around us. People who built their homes near the forest in Kelowna to be close to nature were unprepared for the savagery of uncontrollable fires that destroyed their homes, remarks Percy. I have noticed that the insects and pine needles I track into the house do not want to be swept back out. I have watched warily as one century blends uncomfortably into the next. We are increasingly being invaded by the demands of the developing world: our resources are diminishing, while AIDS, SARS, new cancers, and West Nile virus strike. The pictures of the dispossessed, the victims of wars of greed, invade our television programs as all the refugees cross borders. The world of the other is crossing over into ours. Soon cougars will be crossing the line that I have marked out as my domicile. Soon we will be transformed. Maybe even trade places. Or be slit down the middle, like the whale. Divided in half. This thought frightens me. It makes me realize that all the book learning in the world cannot protect me against this encroachment, this invasion.

Percy defends those who are, like him, untutored. He is especially protective toward adolescent cougars. "I saw an article in *The Province* in May '94 about a cougar killed by an RCMP constable after it attacked a child. I know for a fact that it was very young, I could tell from the picture, and its parents were killed earlier that year around Gold River. Later the constable was himself attacked by a cougar." He smirks derisively as he tells me this.

"Really, it's quite amazing that the first human killed on the island was in 1949, and that was an Indian boy named Dominic Taylor up in Cayugut. Most of the times when cougars attack, it's because the person is doing something fairly stupid. There was the cougar chased back out by a man who had a fish in his hand and was walking a poodle; he shot the cougar that came into his house. Around Ralph River, small dogs were killed at a campsite, but the people had ignored the warnings about cougar sightings. We should not have little dogs we need to protect, but dogs that protect us. Otherwise we are screwing up the natural order.

And people in isolated places need protection. There was no human killed by a cougar on Vancouver Island before 1949."

There is safety in numbers. We need protection. Percy agrees with this much. Yet, like me, he prefers to live alone.

"That's why I usually had around three hounds, in case a cougar decided to fight rather than go up a tree. Most cougar accidents happen in the bush, like that boy killed at Cayugut last year, in the same place an Indian boy was killed in 1949. They should never have been alone. When the boy was found dead next morning, the police said he was killed by a 2-year-old adult, but I doubt that. How could the police know its age? I've been around 500 cougars, but I still can't tell their age from looking at them. Only VERY young ones are distinguishable."

"Once there was a jogger on the highway by the lodge who was chased by a cougar who was jogging too. It stopped when he stopped and would not have hurt him. It was just running because he was running. You have to wonder who was imitating who."

"And then there was that Port Hardy girl being chased by a cougar, and a woman beat it off with a broom. Only sick or half-starved cougars attack. So many people die every day in car accidents, but we accept that. So why can't we accept a very rare human death in the natural world? Like adolescent humans, cougars do stupid things while they are learning. But when cougars do these things, we demand retribution. What if we put a bounty on people for the same reason? Most accidents are due to human error and ignorance."

"You know, predators do not want to fight. People ask silly questions like "If a bear and cougar fight, who would win?" Only sex and food drive them to fight, not like humans. Sometimes I have seen cougars kill their young, no one knows why. But a good hunter said a cougar killed 25 deer in one night. That's impossible, just a tall tale to impress. It would take a cougar at least one hour to stalk and kill each deer. People always want to create bigger stories about cougars."

I always avoid walking along a straight path. Nor do I take the low road, but prefer canyon ridges, looking down upon the activity in the valley. Mine is the middle kingdom, for we are more divine

than humans, more profane than gods. Like me, Percy is a nomad.
Descended from those whiskey Scots, Percy Dewar also chose the
high road. So now we both occupy the crown of creation, for Percy
chose to build his final home -- a huge log house -- at the top of
a mountain across from Strathcona Park Lodge, a place that we
cougars inhabit. A little bit of heaven. Quite a feat for a human
being, coming up to my level. A strenuous one-hour hike up a road
that twists toward the sky. Barely accessible by vehicle, even with
fourwheel drive. Now I can see him even better. I can intuit the
perfect moment, an instant of carelessness by a large animal, and
I can leap from behind, grasp the head in my paws and release my
claws, and twist the neck so easily. But he is different. I will leave
him alone. For now.

"In those days, they used to record the deaths by the skull size, not by their
weight or height. The skull had to be cleaned and dried, and then its score was
a combination of length and width. The largest in the world measured sixteen
inches. From 1870 until 1990, there were 32,662 cougars killed in B.C., and 13,
765 were taken on the island. In 1871, the bounty was ten dollars for each cougar, and it stayed like that until the middle of the Depression, when it went up to
twenty dollars until 1957. Except for a while there in the 40's it was fifteen dollars.
There used to be lots of us cougar hunters. Like Cougar Charlie Caldwell. And
of course Cougar Smith from up around Comox. Cecil was his name. He had
terrible dogs, just got by on a lot of luck, 'cause he bagged a lot of cougars. In the
early days anyone with dogs and a rifle could hunt cougars, they were what the

Ministry of Agriculture called a "noxious pest and varmint predator." But Cecil Smith was the one who inspired Roderick Haig-Brown, who was a good friend of mine. Wrote a book about cougars. And now there's even a provincial park named after him. Just like there's a road named after my family in Nanaimo. Yes, there were lots of cougar hunters in them days. Of course Cougar Annie on the West coast, she was fierce!"

"In June 1949, there was a native kid named Dominic Taylor who was killed on the beach near Kyuquot Reserve between Tofino and Uclulet. My brother Jim came out to hunt that cougar, arrived by float plane, and had it treed within forty minutes. Jim also was the one that taught Cougar Annie how to trap cougars, mostly because she kept bothering him and he didn't like having to travel to remote places that much; he was your typical lazy government employee. But a good hunter. He had a lot of practice, a lot of skill. He told a newspaper reporter in 1959 that, since he killed his first cougar in September 1929, he killed several hundred since, and lost six hounds to the big cats. He was the chief predator hunter hired by the Game Department in 1947 with Bud Frost, from Port Alberni, Ken Moores, and Skate Hames of Courtney, and I guess they were all pretty good hunters, especially my brother. But he never mellowed, believed till the day he died that the only good cougar is a dead cougar. We were pretty opposite brothers in that way. And I guess that never really changed. The only thing that's changed is that there are fewer cougars today. Cougars were all around us at the time."

The cougar is the last large carnivore still numerous and widespread enough to exert an evolutionary influence on its prey. Where natives worshipped the cougar for its hunting prowess, white settlers loathed it for precisely the same reason. In 1771, Linnaeus labeled the cougar *Felix concolor*, the cat of one colour, believing that the North American version was a smaller, more degenerate species of the lion. Many eighteenth century biologists believed that animals and man lived closer together than was true. Theodore Roosevelt, a wildlife enthusiast, found the cougar morally disturbing because it is the deadliest of foes to the most harmless species of wildlife, calling it the "lord of stealthy murder...with a heart both craven and cruel." In the stories of Ambrose Bierce, the cougar is the most Damned Thing. Ernest Thomas Seton called the North American cougar "this glorious exemplar of the laws that made the world."

Lacking archaeological evidence of fossils, observers animalized man even if it required humanizing the animal world, which had previously been regarded as entirely remote from mankind -- man at the top of the vertical ascent of evolution. Now Disney does the same. Civil society has been made entirely by man. So who made the wild? And are we in danger of becoming too civilized, creating a malaise that is slowly killing us? The Body Shop sells a T-shirt that reads "Extinction is forever". A new credo, since it has been found that love is not forever. Now the search for eternal verities leads toward the precipice of death, in search of our wild side.

Percy thinks that he has learned more in one lifetime than many other people.

"Maybe this knowledge is the most important thing I have to pass on. Your life can depend on knowing survival skills." His words make me feel young and small again. He shakes his head sadly, remembering how many friends he has lost to logging and other accidents. "There were real life and death consequences to the kinds of things I was taught. Learning from my mistakes and knowing to be prepared for anything -- those are the two best lessons my dad ever taught me."

Born on June 5, 1919, Percy was close to his father, a Scottish immigrant who taught him a love of animals; together, they raised goats, chickens and dogs during the Depression. "When I went walking with my Dad in the evenings, it was possible to count up to 80 deer in one hour. My Dad taught me how to notice animal habits, keep my eyes open always." He also learned how to build from his father, who helped build the Government road. One of the first things his father taught him, after learning how to care for animals, was how to build chicken houses for their chicken farm, and to cut cedar shakes.

"My mother liked to garden, and we preserved a lot of food. Even during the Depression, we had it relatively easy, and we always ate well. Each of the children in our family was given a section of the garden plot to tend, and this became a source of competition and of pride. Pleasure came from work. I still do not understand why people want to be entertained. They want to pay forty dollars for a hockey ticket and eight dollars to park, but demand higher wages than their labour is worth. I was taught to pick up pennies, but people today find it too much of an effort to stoop down to do so. "Waste not, want not" is a maxim that was part of our upbringing. And gathering food for the family was a great source of both pride and fun. My earliest memory is of trout fishing the Benson Creek near Extension in the early mornings, waiting for my mother to signal us from a distance with a white dish towel that it was time to go to school."

Percy's grandfather was killed in a brewery accident in Sterling, Scotland, when his father was only four years old, so Percy only heard stories about him and his love of greyhounds and horses. Percy's father kept his name even though he had a stepfather after he died. This is something that Percy is proud of today, as he refers to a book about the history of the distilling of scotch: the Dewar family tradition of making scotch is a long and famous one, founded by Percy's great great grandfather. To use one of his father's favourite expressions, Percy describes him as the kind of humourous, honest man "who would give a cat's ass heartburn" -- a helpful, blunt, and strong-willed man. His mentor.

His mother's parents were already in Ladysmith when the Dewars moved to Canada in 1914, and like many other labourers, traveled to the coalmines by train. Percy's elder siblings were born in Scotland, and he comes from what he calls "a good-sized family" of ten children (seven boys and three girls), who lived on far end of Extension, close to Mount Benson. It seems fitting that Percy, who has always lived on the edge of things, should have his beginnings in Extension, beyond the city limits, at the border between places. All his real transformations seem to occur at frontiers.

Like his father, all the children played soccer, a tradition brought from Scotland. He has a brother in Vancouver whom he has seen little of in the past twenty years, since Percy rarely leaves the island. Percy's eldest sister Anne, to whom he is closest, lives in Parksville, where she keeps track of other family members. Percy has always been more interested in animals than human beings. And, he says, they are not a close family. He maintains that Scots are selfish. Six months could go by before he hears from his brother, and he does not care. Like Percy, Anne is well off and lives very comfortably, but disdains money. The only other surviving sister, two years younger than Percy and also a widow, lives in Kelowna. She had a pub in Abbotsford, and worked hard all her life. Hard work is what kept all his family members alive so long, Percy claims. Certainly he looks several decades younger than his eighty years.

"We had this work ethic instilled in us at a young age. My sister, who commanded us kids around like an army sergeant, scrubbed floors for an elderly neighbour woman every Saturday, even when I was very small. I was also asked to chop the week's kindling and haul water from the well for her. One day this widow gave each of us fifty cents, and it made my mother angry that we accepted money from a neighbour, so we had to take the money back to her. Never take money for helping people, she said. Anyway, what I learned from my childhood is that it is best to keep busy all the time, and more fun than being idle. Never been one for just sitting around."

"One thing I remember really clearly when I was growing up was the time I went to see an old character named Joe di Rosa, who came from Corsica. He really scared me when he told me what was going to happen to me. Nobody in the village of Extension respected him that much because he was drunk most of the time, except that he was a remarkably good psychic. He refused to read the palms of two of the boys I knew because of what he saw in them; both of these fellows died before they turned thirty. He read my palm and told me that I would never be short of money and would have plenty of women. Because I was so young and shy, this was not something I wanted to think about, and that's the part that scared me." Percy laughs gently and his eyes sparkle when he tells me this. He fancies himself a bit of a ladies' man, an irony given his penchant for avoiding people.

Percy denies having any superstition, and maintains that he doesn't know one religion from another. "I never could believe in it or why it existed. My mother was religious, but my father was not. He was raised United. There were two churches in the village in Extension, and one was Catholic; it never had its windows broken, but the other one did, so I knew that Catholic boys were up to no good. But to me it makes no sense that there's a god up there; even if there were, can you imagine him coming down to judge people as either good or bad? And I don't believe in reincarnation neither. There is just no justice in our world, and it is foolish to apply such concepts to the animal world, as foolish as it is to romanticize Indians or commercial fisherman."

He is talking to me about his ideas about religion while he is showing me how to make a "bug". "No sense in being idle while we talk," he repeats often. A "bug" is a candle to get you through the woods at night, constructed by hooking a coat hanger through a tin can, punching holes in it, and placing a candle inside. He seems amazed that I do not know how to make one, and patiently shows me. We get back to the topic of religion.

"We are guided by instinct," he says. "But human beings forget this, ignore it all the time, even have to be retaught how to use it. Animals don't have to be taught these instincts. The way they scent their prey or pinpoint a sound, all the movements of the hunters and the hunted are, in a way, a part of an animal's hunting life, just background knowledge, and knowing all these details is a matter of survival. An animal's interests lie in learning hunting techniques whether they are immediately useful or not, and using them is equally natural. They enjoy them, and when they've had enough to eat they go to sleep, or when they're hungry, they feed. I think cougars develop a map of the country in their brains, a very detailed and complete one, that they use again and again." And Percy remains curious about how they are born with such knowledge, the only mystery that he will concede. "Life is to be faced. Do what there is to do. The only question to ask is, 'Should I be doing this at all?' Was there ever a time he was scared, I ask? "Never." But his halo is a bit askew as he says this. A fighter who respects his opponent, admires adaptability, he is confident and cocksure. Cougars are actually a peaceful adversary, as long as you leave them alone, Percy insists. Great trackers are formed by great intuition, and instinctively hit upon the line the animal is most likely to follow, then move on until another sign confirms the hunch, he tells me. The best way to hunt is to travel the same route over and over again in a circuit, wait for the cougar to come to you. Good trackers track by eye as much as possible, before releasing the hounds. "The point is to surprise the cougar, not let the baying give advance warning."

> *If you leave me wounded in the woods, I become an outlaw too. I*
> *am only marginalized after you have crippled me. So I will double*
> *back and forth across every river to confuse my pursuers. If you fall*
> *on my track when I am myself tracking prey, I can promise you a*

long day rambling along a crooked path. And I will never give you
a predictable circuit that you can interpret. You call me an enigma,
but the heart of the enigma is your own confusion.

After finishing grade eight in Extension in a one-room schoolhouse with about twenty-five children, Percy found that there was nowhere to go to school. No one in his family completed school beyond eighth grade. The wagon road leading to Nanaimo, the closest place to attend high school, was simply too long to travel every day, and too full of ruts for Percy to ride his bicycle along. He likes to brag that in elementary school, he did his homework quickly in the hallway, never having to take it home, and then picked it up in the morning so that he could walk the four miles after school to play soccer without having to carry all his books. He generally reached home after dark. When his teacher urged him to stay and study after school instead, he said "No way, I am going to play soccer." Percy was clearly defiant from an early age.

"I guess it would have been wise to continue with school, but it was not possible. I was glad to finish at that school. I had to go to Nanaimo for the final exam, and I scored well, the highest of the three kids who went."

And he loved to roam the woods by himself. I think of him walking miles alone every day, well into the dark, and I think of how strictly accompanied my children are escorted safely through every day of their lives. Boundaries and rules strictly maintained. Brochures on "stranger-proofing" my children arrive home in their backpacks. They rarely stray more than a couple of blocks from home, and are required to come and ask my permission before they do so. My own childhood was wilder, and I spent hours in the woods building a tree fort with my friends or wandering the trails on foot or by bike. Was the world safer then? I don't think so. Perhaps we have just become more paranoid. Percy agrees with me. He also says that, when he was growing up, there were some bad people but everyone knew who they were. It was impossible to live in a small place like Extension and not know everything about everyone else, he says.

One of Percy's first hunting cabins

His brother Jim had a hound first. At the age of sixteen, Percy got his first hound, and this he describes as one of the most joyous moments of his life. "I didn't know how to train it for cougar, which is hard and long, especially keeping them from chasing other animals who leave their scents in the woods too. By the time I had my third hound, I'd worked out how I could hunt cougar on bare ground with no snow. You have to see the track so you would know you were tracking a cougar and not something else. Most hounds would be able to pick up the scent but the hunter can't trust them without seeing the tracks in the snow. I caught on quick. After that, it got easier. An older, more reliable dog could be loose and ranging back and forth, and the others would walk behind until the leader found the scent and started baying. Then they would go to help the lead dog. As they got better trained, I would alternate dogs, letting each one be the leader for about an hour so they all had a turn. Of course cougars can easily outrun dogs, sometimes even retracing their tracks or stopping casually, as if to say "Just dare try to catch me!" And you have to remember how important it is to have fresh, alert dogs. Tired dogs will never tree a cougar, and you can tell from their baying, if it gets kind of weary and ragged-like. A cougar will hardly tree even before a fresh dog, unless they come upon him suddenly, usually when he is heavy with meat and dazed from gorging and sleeping. He will turn his head and look calmly back to the sound of the hounds coming, and sometimes snarl or lay his ears back flat as his eyes get all fierce. Then he crouches, looks up at the top of the tree, and works his paws against the ground as if he were about to spring a deer. Then he leaps and his claws grip the bark of the tree trunk, springing up the tree instead of climbing it like a bear would – it's quite amazing to see!"

"In the thirties, and right up to the sixties, there were vast areas of mature timber, so when you trailed a cougar you had to stay overnight because there were no roads to lead you out. We often stayed in primitive cabins, some of which we built ourselves, or some of which were just anybody's for the taking. I remember one of them near Jack Creek from 1949.

Tracking sometimes took 9 to 10 hours. You let your dogs rest at night. Sitting there before the fire, even though you are cold and tired, you have the dogs around you and you feel peaceful and good. I know I have had a very lucky life, mostly because I have always had excellent hounds."

Cougar in tree

Percy cut firewood by hand and sold it, although he made hardly any money. "But then a dollar a day seemed like a lot. The government gave my brother a six-month trial job, and I persuaded him to include me as his partner. The contract, arranged by the Maffeo family, stipulated that if we caught six cougars within six months, my brother would be given a permanent job. That's how he became the first permanent predator hunter on the island and worked for Fish and Wildlife until he died at the age of sixty-one. Between us two boys, we caught seventeen cougars during the trial period." He admits that the experience was the beginning of a life long desire to learned more about cougars. They piqued his interest for a number of reasons. "It was because they were so difficult. So mysterious. I was trying to find out what I could about them, and they made it challenging. You spend you life near something and you don't know anything about it." He also bonded with the solitary animals. "I spent most of my life alone. I felt very close to the cougars. Cougars are private from each other and from humans. Privacy means a lot to them, since that is how they survive. They hunt to stay alive."

"I always believed that if you could not do something well, there was no sense in doing it at all. So I made sure I got good at everything I did."

"I felt the freedom and excitement of working with hounds, and it never left me. I tracked moose or caribou up north, which seemed dull by comparison. I was very proud of my hounds. Most cougar guides only tracked cougar over snow, but I trained my Blue Tick hounds to locate and track in summer too, when there were no snow tracks to follow. The only time those dogs got a rest was when it rained. You cannot follow a cougar scent in the rain. One time a bear charged my brother when we were walking a narrow trail in standing timber. He was walking ahead with the dogs, and I was packing the gun in behind him. My brother yelled for me to kill it. I was sixteen at the time but done a good job on it."

"Another bear story for you: The people at the weather station on Hope Island – that's off the top end of Vancouver Island – reported seeing a cougar, so we went up there. There were no roads, so they were making a sidewalk one mile long. The bears all used the new sidewalk. It was blueberry season, so they left many piles of poop. One morning I got up early and stuck pieces of toilet paper on some of the piles. The crew nearly went on strike, saying they wouldn't build the sidewalk until the weather station people changed their habits."

"In 1934, I built a cabin, about ten by sixteen feet, in the woods for our hunts, just using what scraps were in the woods. We acted as if we owned the trees and split the boards. Every teen knew how to build a cabin in the woods. Once I had my own hounds, I would go out in the bush every weekend. I did not always get to a cabin before dark so I would start looking for fire material an hour or so before dusk in winter. One time I had a good fire going, and my dogs had gone over the mountain so I couldn't hear them and decided to wait until morning as I still had two young pups with me. But all of a sudden a cougar leapt out at the pups. I didn't think, just kicked it in the rear end and it left. The next morning I could see from the tracks in the snow that it had sat on the log for a long time watching the pups and me before it made the leap at the dogs. There was always enough deer meat for the dogs, and we would catch ten or twelve fish a day. That's how I got started, really. And it was always hard work - living away all winter in cabins, with no proper clothing. We'd get up at daylight and leave with the dogs, usually getting back after dark, mostly on snowshoes in the winter months. Once three bull elk attacked me in big old growth timber; the dogs came to me for help, and I had to run from tree to tree. Eventually the elks seemed to tire of the game and left me alone."

"But I learned a lot, and I enjoyed it -- the challenge of learning how to hunt. I felt lucky and successful. When the dogs start in on a cougar track, you have to go! The scent stays for days in the snow, and at times you have to cross a river or large creeks or look for a large tree to get across, and those trees can be as slippery as greased owl shit. When you have to stay outside overnight so you don't lose the trail, the thing to do is to look for a fir snag with the bark coming off. I always packed pitch with me so I could start a fire that would last all night. Hunting has changed so much now, though, and often hunters don't even track the animals. Hunting today means riding in your fourwheel drive, and shooting from the road."

Percy thought well of himself, believing he was some kind of a hero. His main idol was the cougar hunter called Cougar Charlie (Charlie Caldwell), who convinced him that, when it came to hunting, you cannot learn enough about it in a lifetime. Certainly weekender bounty hunters were not as experienced as those who made it their full-time occupation, nor did they know their hounds as well. Cougar Charlie made good home brew, and refused to work for wages, living on what he earned from his hides, and what he ate from his garden. His other hero was his namesake Percy Sutton, who worked for the Fire Patrol in Nanaimo.

"Because we had the same name, he was like my double and I spent a lot of time learning from him. I got three lifetimes' worth of knowledge passed on to me from Percy Sutton. Many of the others made mistakes, but he was the best." Great trackers are formed by great intuition, since they seem to hit instinctively upon the line an animal is likely to follow and to move on until seeing another sign to confirm their initial hunch. From this man, Percy learned to how to notice tracks and footprints in puddles.

Percy Sutton, who was in his forties when the fifteen-year-old boy met him, never married, choosing to spend his lifetime in the woods. Percy learned bachelorhood from him. "Some people should not be married, and I'm one of those types. Maybe you are too," he tells me. The elder Percy became a substitute father for him, and tirelessly answered all his questions. He was quiet and thoughtful, teaching Percy and his brother what he knew about hunting. Percy says that Sutton's dogs were not well-trained, but that he taught him to learn from his mistakes, summarizing what he had learned painstakingly from trial and error. Like Percy's own father, this man emphasized how to be more observant.

> *So how is it that you have learned so little of what I have taught*
> *you? I left you the entrails of my slaughtered deer for you to read,*
> *but you ignored them. Only one or two of you quiet ones were wor-*
> *thy to be my disciples. Now where have you gone?*

"Sutton trapped from an early age, never did anything else except patrol for fire for the E & N Railway. In those days, there were just trails, no roads, and the logging was just by the railroad. People walked everywhere, and kept the trails open in case of fire. He worked for no one else, was quiet, kept to himself."

"Percy Sutton lived in the woods, often in a snow house around the Nanaimo Lakes area, a region he knew very well. He had all the answers, never said 'I don't know'. He had two wire-haired terriers, and he certainly got his use out of them. Somehow he got on salary throughout the Depression, which was quite an amazing feat during them days. Percy knew a lot about wildlife, and he passed that on to me, for free. What an education I got from that man!"

I tell Percy that I once read that the Inuit believe that if an animal does something unusual in your presence, you should take it personally, since of course animals are superior beings with whom we can have close relationships. Animals are seen as role models and avatars of personalities from former lives. I explain to him what "avatar" means when he asks, and then he tells me more animal stories.

Once Percy made friends with a wounded deer, took it home and nursed it back to health. "When you live out in the woods, you see wonderful things: when deer are just about to give birth, they chase all the fawns away. Sometimes the mother returns later. When the fawns are on their own, they seem unsure what to do. I saw a two-year-old travel with a large buck watching from a distance. When they were crossing the river, which was about 2 feet deep, the buck crossed with one fawn and came back for the one that did not want to cross, forcing it to wade through the water by rubbing against it. In mid-June, you will always see more deer than any other time of year, and they communicate more with each other then."

Once Percy lost a four-year-old dog near Gold River when a cougar got it as it slid down a slope. Percy took his sweater and wrapped it around the dog, sleeping against a tree until morning when he could pack it further and bring it home by seaplane. I close my eyes to imagine this strange pieta.

I first revealed myself to Percy when he reached the age of fifteen. The border between boyhood and manhood. He usually describes places in terms of the age of the trees, so he says he saw me in an area that was all mature timber, between three small, noisy rivers, at a south fork in the Nanaimo River. He makes it a landmark. A landscape so clear that it is crystalline in memory all these years later. At the time, he was with his brother and two hounds, and couldn't hear the dogs as they were crossing the river on poles. He describes the moment as thrilling, but insists that he was not afraid. Later at Cowichan Lake, near the railroad, he told Cougar Charlie excitedly that it was female because of its small head, and that, although it was dark and the cougar was a mile away by then, he was certain he could find it. "I can't see so good, boy. I've only got three shells. Do you think you can shoot it?" asked Cougar Charlie. "Charlie would've killed me if I missed it, Percy was heard to brag later to his friends. "So I made sure I didn't."

I let him have the first few cougars. Let him think that he was boss. Let him deny fear itself. The young are so cocky.

But at least he is not arrogant. You say you want to know me because I am savage. Time must be found. Patience must be cultivated. You need experience if you want to trace me. Learn to wait. Pray for luck. You need to both fear me and sympathize with me. Do not be fastidious or squeamish. If you love comfort too much, or are unprepared to follow where I lead, you will never know me. You must have total personal commitment, and some pride. This is how Percy and I recognized each other. Be fearless. A man becomes arrogant when he is armed. Thinks himself Master of Creation. Abandon your guns, traps, collars, cages. I would prefer to meet you without any metal between us. How can you be at peace with yourself when you carry a weapon of destruction? Rather focus your faculties on a quiet pursuit of knowledge and then you will see that, like a housecat, I will come to you. You will first have to listen to your own fears in the dark for many hours. I will retreat into deep forest, not attracting attention. Observe, do not capture. Live with me as a fellow being. Share my wilderness. Ignore the rumours of my being a mankiller. You are the mankiller. You do not suit my taste buds. You are not normal prey.

So, tonight, attune yourself to sights and sounds and smells. Time passes slowly when you stand vigil in the dark of night. The moon is alive, has features you have never seen before.

I ask Percy what kept him motivated in the 20's and 30's, and he says it was the personal challenge to do the best that he could. He spent most of his time enjoying the wildlife, and learning better ways to do things in a new territory.

"If a weekend of hunting was coming up, there was always the excitement of planning for it. And oh, God, what a thrill it was to hear the hounds baying and to be tuned in to them! It was the best thing in my whole life! In the early mornings, the dogs would set out, one out ahead with his nose to the ground and his tail in the air. His first bark would signal the other hounds that they were allowed to join him. He would start barking as soon as he caught the scent, then bay more as the scent improved and he would speed up. I can almost hear the dogs bawling on the back side of a bluff, seeing a disturbance on the trail. And when the dog would stand at the foot of the tree, all four legs braced almost as if against the recoil of his voice, his head raised a little, he would have his mouth side open and just pour forth this continuous loud volume of melody, like a song to my ears, anyway. He never took his eyes off of that cougar! I had another hound that would dance on its toes, barking and barking, shaking all eagerly and from fear, no doubt. And sometimes he'd just stop for a moment and sit, head cocked to one side, looking up, as if he didn't quite believe he was capable of making so much noise, or couldn't understand why the cougar wouldn't just give up. You can really hear the difference in their baying as soon as they pick up the scent of the cougar on the trail, boy! And it makes you get all excited just like the dogs. If a snow track is melted by the sun, then freezes, it is hard for the dogs to pick up the scent. But when it thaws slightly, the smell is clear. Then you need to interpret the signs."

"I had only one hound during the war years. We hunted raccoon for six dollars each. This was illegal, but I had a permit from Eaglecrest farms, where they raised turkeys and chickens. Mostly I hunted them between Parksville and Qualicum, and I really enjoyed working with the dog. At this job, I worked nights for four years from 10 p.m. until 3 a.m., which is the best time to catch them. The time between night and day. Then I went to work in the mornings in logging."

"Most of all I enjoyed how the dog worked; he was named Pilot and he was my first dog. One night I went hunting with two other guys and their dogs. My dog was barking at the bottom of the tree, so high up the tree he couldn't smell anything any more. That was a good dog, to be able to locate one tree among so many old growth timbers. He barked one hour, was really insistent, when all the others wanted to give up. Of course, it wasn't their dog, so they didn't care! Sure enough, there was a coon at the top of a huge Douglas fir; we saw its eyes at last. That was my very first hound, and those were really fun times."

"Good dogs are scarce. You've got to live with a dog every day to train it properly. Mine lived longer than most. They always had that will to go." Restlessness and longevity combined. Of the three dogs that were ten years old at the beginning of the seven-year cougar study he initiated, all remained alive until the end of the study, in spite of predictions from outsiders that none would stay the course.

Blue Tick hounds are the best breed for dedication, loyalty, longevity, patience, and endurance. Percy tells me that his favourite dog was named Lou, and he had her during the 1960's.

They can distinguish the scent of cougar or raccoon from other animal scents, and not chase after deer, if taught properly. Like the hunter, they need swift feet, good stamina, and a loud, clear voice. He shows me his technique for training dogs not to hunt deer: he built a cone-shaped wire cage which turns like a cement mixer, in which he places a deer carcass in the cage and turns the dog in it, to make the animal dizzy and associate the smell of deer with unpleasant sensations. "You've got to break him off deer and coon if he'll be any good to you in this country. They need to be disciplined, just like children." Shuddering, I wonder what the S.P.C.A. would make of such a contraption. Kind to be cruel sometimes, says Percy. Clearly he is a man obsessed.

His reputation for training hounds and for guiding spread by word of mouth, as Percy received publicity for capturing cougars that were stalking wildlife. "I learned that the best months for sighting cougar were May, June, and July. Guiding is difficult, especially because you are stuck with those people for twenty-four hours a day. I was not like other guides, who just dump tourists off at the motel and then pick them up in the morning. I was very particular about who I took out with me, mostly people who wanted to shoot pictures, not animals. I still maintain that all hunting should be stopped completely. Because I had hounds, I could take people out at any time of the year. Few other guides could do this. I refused to take one government hunter from the Fraser Valley out unless he left his dogs behind. I amazed him by showing him that my hounds did not chase deer;

he had never bothered to train his own dogs that well. He'd been trying to catch a cougar for two years, but when he was out with me, he caught one on the first day."

Training hounds since 1950, he says he has always done it for pleasure, never for profit. People who mix dogs and money too much end up bad, he insists. "I only guided to cover my expenses, not to make a profit. I had an income from leasing the land. I had clients from Ontario, Manitoba, Georgia, even the editor of *Outdoor Life*, and the guy who invented the tranquilizer gun. Eventually people as far away as California inquired about "that cougar man Percy" and his brother, through Fish & Wildlife, and hired me as a guide. Once a college group from Ohio hired me to take them out from Qualicum Bay, two at a time, renting a hotel for some months. Most of the students were quite lazy. They thought that 'manual labour' was the name of a Mexican! I was considered heroic. But I was just doing something that very few other people did and that this earned me a reputation.

> *As if there were such a thing as being a hero. When we all come to the same end. When your neck could snap easily. One twist, and cougarman Percy would be just a man again. But he pleased me and therefore I honoured him with knowledge of me. Go forth and teach them to protect my young when I am gone, for without them, I am nothing.*

Still playing the maverick, Percy took on the forest as a practice foe before he took on Fish and Wildlife, or stray photojournalists, later in his life. He likes to remind me that he has never had a regular job, even in logging. A mask of pride covers his face.

"During the time I logged, I also trapped marten for money, usually all day Sundays and on Wednesday nights, earning more trapping than logging during those years. But I could not quit logging, since regular jobs were hard to come by and everyone's work was frozen during the war. As soon as the war was over, I quit that logging job. I had to stick with logging during the war. It was either that or go into the army. I didn't even know any Germans, let alone feel mad enough to shoot one. I was not that kind of person. And I never liked social life. I was working in a logging camp when war broke out, and we heard about it on the radio in September, 1939. For all of us, it was not a nice feeling. I like my country but I am not willing to go fight for it. I know what wars are about: some people get very rich by them, not that they take the risk of killing or being killed themselves."

In 1940, Percy had just started a job at a brand new camp, and left Lake Cowichan to go to work. By 1942, when the call for conscription came, the logging camp got him a deferment from the army. Meanwhile, in 1941, he purchased 12 acres in Parksville, behind the present SaveOn Foods, for which he paid $275; the lot had one house on it. After the war ended, Percy sold the 12 acres for $2500. "That's what started me having a bit of money," he says.

In 1946, he also purchased another property in Extension from a man named Marshall, a fellow for whom he'd done a lot of favours as a kid. Now a pensioner, Marshall insisted that Percy buy the place, so Marshall himself could move in with his daughter in Chase River. Marshall owned four lots, with a large old seven-room house set in the field. When Percy insisted more fiercely that he didn't even want it, Marshall told him that he was, by the terms of his pension, only allowed to sell it for 300 dollars, and said he'd keep after Percy until he bought it. Although Percy had the money, and Marshall kept pestering him until he bought it, he was reluctant to make the purchase because of the fact that it seemed like a lot of money to him at the time. Shortly after he bought the place, he became aware that Fish & Wildlife needed a place for predator control, so Percy leased part of property to them for 17 years. There were no hunters during the war, as most of the men were away, so the property was used by Percy's brother, who was in charge of raising Fish & Wildlife tracking dogs there. His brother hired 3 other men: Aubrey Hanes, Bud Frost, and Ken Moores. "The other two started late in their lives. Hanes was the best predator hunter; he knew what he was doing. He is still alive now, in his eighties, and I visit him from time to time."

Percy advanced quickly in logging, although work was not steady on a year-round basis -- either it was too hot or too cold. "I was the head loader, so I selected the logs to go on the truck, where they would go, and I ran the loading machine. I worked on the first shovel that loaded logs. I worked with some old time hook tenders – that's the guy who's in charge of a crew of about ten men, and usually the crews were working pretty far apart – and they were great at splicing and getting so much power out of the machine. Those old characters loved passing ideas on to young guys like me who were keen to learn. One tough old Scot told one of the crew guys who had been off sick and not figured out why he was sick that, back in Scotland, the Highland doctors would have you shit on a kale leaf and then tell you the disease and the cure. Another hook tender I worked with at Cowichan Lake was a great beer drinker named Bob. He would get in terrible fights and not always win, so when he came to, he would go back the guy's house and start the fight all over again. One time Bob got the best of the other guy, who could not stand, so Bob picked him up and hung him on the fence by his suspenders and really worked him over. Then he just left him hanging there on the fence!"

"The older guys liked to pull jokes on the young ones. At that time, they worked six days a week, and sometimes a holiday came, so you could get a three-day weekend. So I was headed home for three days, and this guy asked me would I mail a letter for him. I said sure, so he came back with the letter and asked me did I know the difference between a mailbox and an elephant's ass? I didn't want to spoil his joke, so I said I didn't. Then he said, "Never mind, I'll mail it myself." They always done these things when there was a whole group of guys standing around, to make you look really bad. All the guys liked me, though. Hardboiled loggers gave me jobs at twenty years old that others couldn't handle till they were forty. I guess I also told good stories, and that pleased them."

"At one time, loggers all stayed in camps. In October or November, a salesman would come around to the camps and measure people for a suit for the Christmas shutdown. Most everyone went to Vancouver for a big time, spending as long as the money lasted. One man, another Scot, wore Stanfields underwear, like most men. When the time come to go to town, he just put his suit on top of his wool underwear. After that they called him Dirty Shirt. And he was a rough kind. But he was an easygoing hook tender where some were not. Once I watched him pick up a dusty grapefruit dropped by a truck driver, and he scooped out its insides with his buck teeth.

"I knew a rigger named Dan who always drank too much on Saturday nights and had a short fuse. If he couldn't get his thermos open, he smashed it on a rock. I also watched him smash his watch because it felt to him like time was passing too slowly. A few years later, that kind of anger got him killed: he drove from Kelsey Bay to Campbell River in a heavy rain storm, the water was up over the bridge on Salmon river, and when he walked on the bridge to check it out because he was too impatient to wait out the storm, the bridge went out, so he went down with it and drowned."

"An older fellow named Bill lived on garlic. He used to get on the bus in the mornings, and one time the driver was so knocked out by the garlic smell that he stopped the bus, thinking that the brakes were on fire. One of the meanest men was named Olson, and I even got along with him; he told me I was the most even tempered guy he had ever worked with."

"The logging camp shut down the day the war ended, so that everyone could enjoy a huge celebration. I felt only a sense of relief." Casually he mentions that he got married at the beginning of the war, which "served its purpose in keeping me at home"; by the end of the war, the marriage had ended. Reluctant to discuss this episode in his life, Percy makes it clear he would rather talk about hounds than about personal relationships.

"I got married at 21, but it didn't last; she went back home. I guess I married on an impulse, to avoid going into the army. It served its purpose. I knew Frances from the village of Extension and from school; everybody there knew everybody else all their lives. We got married at a church in the south end of Nanaimo called Haliburton Free Church, just the immediate family, and I did not much enjoy the wedding. I think I was maybe trying to save her from her alcoholic family. But I guess I was not the marrying type, and I think you have got to live with someone first before you know if you can stand them." Silently, I concur with him. I have been married three times, and I must not be the marrying type either. Three strikes and you're out.

After the war, divorce was very common, Percy states, and so it was easy for him to obtain the services of "that Brother Twelve lawyer -- you know him. He is the same guy who married me the second time around too," he laughs. Percy's first wife is dead now; she died of alcoholism, although she did not drink when Percy met her, nor during their marriage. What drove her to drink later on? I ask him. He shrugs his shoulders.

> *My mate is gone now. He lingered around me for a couple of weeks after our six days of furious copulation, sometimes forty times a day. Every time he mounted me, he gnawed my neck in a jaw lock. It only appeared affectionate, and his roughness made me snarl in irritation, flatten my ears. When he got down off me, I would swirl around and swat him in the face with my claws. But even after all our displays, he left me after two weeks, the peak of his social tolerance. I wonder if I will encounter him again. Of course he will not participate in raising the kittens he has sired. And we will maintain a mutually respectful distance. But I will intuit his presence, his smell, sight his tracks and remember this time in my life.*

"What were the most significant moments in my life? Well, I won the splicing championship at logger sports. I was the Canadian champion for four years straight. I always had an interest in splicing wire rope so I became quite good at it."

"But there is nothing like the sound of those dogs baying, how they never get tired, just keep pushing you on and challenging you to be more than you are. That is definitely the highlight of my life."

In this free time, Percy decided to build a house, working at night and on weekends. He did this for all of 1948, completing it in one year, he announces proudly. He claims he "had it easy" at his daytime job, where he manned a log-loading machine on auto-pilot and then had time to think through his building plan all day. After work, Percy took a bus to and from the worksite to Nanaimo, stopping to eat anywhere he chose. He bought a lot for $200 in Five Acres (present day Harewood), which was just beginning to be divided into lots. "Five Acres was known as the poor part of town then, because only poor people had only five acres of land."

Percy did everything himself in constructing the house: poured the cement for the basement, installed the septic tank and plumbing, while a friend did the wiring. He taught himself plumbing by reading books. Today he says that plastic pipes, that do not corrode, are probably the biggest boon to the modern homesteader. By his estimates, the house cost him $2500, and he sold it for $5000, meanwhile earning nine dollars a day logging. (Percy has kept his old pay stubs and shows them proudly to me). Percy now had enough money to take the next year off so that he could be with the hounds. Hunting in the woods was the life he loved most.

> And still you do not know me. Guardian spirit, friend, enemy. You are never certain. My presence, even when I am invisible, will haunt you all the days of your life. My life sustains yours. Will you exploit or worship me? You may achieve success, but you know in your heart that it is fragile. Like the edge of this cliff. See how the rocks tumble below and the edge disintegrates when I claw the

ground. What kind of animal am I, you ask? The kind that deserves respect. The kind that is best left alone.

I watched you study the entrails of a carcass as if divining the signs for meaning. As if you might understand me that way. You cannot know me by what I consume. And I live from feast to famine. Close your eyes and dream of me, a sleek animal tracking through unblemished snow. I have a quest too. Perhaps we are just friends who have never met. I will return your gaze without giving any sign of recognition. I am sensitive to movement and light, but not to colour. I have peripheral vision, which gives me an advantage over prey. Hunters have keener binocular vision to detect shape. Prey have a better chance at escape and survival, while hunters have to work harder to survive. So is it fair to talk about a balance between hunter and prey? Prey must stay alert. At any moment, where prey are lying or feeding or traveling, the hunter may be silently stalking them. So they remain careful, and are given keen ears, keen eyes, keen noses. Yet I must learn to hunt food over a larger range, while prey need only feast on the food of an area known intimately. Prey know the location of shelters. I have no intimacy with geography, must study the habits of my prey, who are my life; where they go, I must follow. Learn by trial and error until I succeed in killing my quarry. Some days I give up in defeat and chase after less alert, less experienced prey.

Being a pacifist during the war made Percy unpopular. He was relieved to have a good paying job, one that he stayed with after the war. Working only eight months of the year provided him with a lot of free time. "Now they have winter equipment to log in the snow, whereas we were just laid off every winter -- not that I minded. And there was no unemployment insurance in those days either." In 1948, the B.C. government hired four full-time hunters to wipe out the cougar and wolf populations on Vancouver Island. The bounty had been on for a long time, and wasn't cancelled, nor the hunters recalled, until the 1950's. In 1950, Percy quit working for MacMillan-Bloedel, and began working for himself. He took out three packs of lumber. Although there was no money in it, the work came easily to him because he was an experienced builder. Percy took down the house he grew up in at the far end of Extension, and used the recycled materials to build a barn in 1955.

He also built a smaller house for his aging parents, but his father died at Christmas, two months before it was completed, although his mother was able to occupy it.

It was the first electrically-heated house in Nanaimo, Percy tells me proudly. He has since built ten other houses, perfecting his building skills each time.

On the lower level of the house, there is a greenhouse heated by the hot water pipes, so that he can enjoy melons and tomatoes in the middle of winter. He looks proud when I compliment him on his brilliant design.

He worked next for a MacMillan Bloedel contractor named Bob Moffit, who paid him a higher wage than he had received as a company man. Bob was very good to Percy because he was so pleased with his work. In 1957, there were crew cutbacks, and although Percy was not expected to give up his job, he volunteered to be laid off first so he could have more time with the hounds. A man at British Ropes asked Percy to help start up its Nanaimo operation, so he worked there for about a year. "The windows were about 12 feet off the ground, so I built a ladder so I could see out and I kept staring out the windows at the mountains."

"Those mountains looked so good that in March I gave two weeks' notice. The manager told me he should never have let me build that ladder." Next Empire Stevedoring asked him to do splicing, and that work suited him as he worked half time, mostly in the winter. "I stayed there for six years, and they didn't want me to leave." The mask of pride stretches across his face again.

"Everybody knew what a good worker I was, and they always asked me back. I was not the kind of person to work for other people forever. From October to May, I stayed at the first Strathcona Lodge, which was empty in winter. I spent most of my time hunting and guiding the people I kept there."

"At that time, there was no road to the lodge, and the only access was from the privately owned Sutherland cabins. Across from them I could row one mile to the lodge. After fall the lake froze over, so then you had to cross by snowshoe. Or you could walk up the old railroad tracks, leftover from when they logged this area during the war. It was a lush area, after having been logged. I haven't seen much elk since that time, except one in the bog down by the highway that must have walked across the highway bridge, a couple years back."

"I stayed at the very first lodge on the original Upper Campbell Lake, and it belonged to a man named Whittaker, who was not the original owner either. He gave me free board just so as to have someone watch over the place in winter. I used to love coming up here, rarely saw anyone else. So I did that for three winters. B.C. Hydro bought the property with the lodge on it, and Wallace Bakkie bought the lodge, put it on cedar logs, and floated it up the lake to its present site. That one burned down. Wallace had several lots up here, and made it a tourist lodge, putting lots of money into it. His daughter Merna and her husband Jim, both schoolteachers, had the idea of turning it into an outdoor education centre. They put thousands of kids through that place, a couple hundred a week from spring until October. That was years later. But only a couple of people wintered there at first. Winters there were quiet, magical. God, it was a beautiful place."

"But my life wasn't always easy, because now I had to deal with people all the time. And guiding is difficult; you're stuck with those people for twenty-four hours a day. I was not like other guides who dump tourists in a motel, and then pick them up every morning." Percy could take tourists out into the backwoods hunting at any time of the year because he had the hounds, whereas few other guides could. "Once there was a government hunter from the Fraser valley who was frustrated because after two years, he had still not caught a cougar. I refused to take him out hunting, but then finally agreed to only if he left his dogs behind and used mine. And of course, he got one on the first day, when he was using my hounds. That's how good my dogs were! He was an ignorant man who had never put in enough time training his dogs not to chase deer."

Percy enjoyed living at the lodge. It was nine miles to Buttle Lake, along an old growth timber trail, and to hear his hound Buckey's voice echo through the woods along that trail was ecstasy to Percy. "It is important that you hear them, since you can't see the cougar or anything else ahead of you, and you just have to trust them and follow. You need a lot of patience with dogs and cougars. You cannot go down the ridge side of the canyon until you can hear your dogs coming up the other side."

"I guided only to cover expenses, since I had an income from leasing the land, and was not interested in profit. I also had money from the sale of my house." Again his reputation spread, and people came from Manitoba, Ontario, and the States. They had heard of his hunting and guiding abilities through word of mouth, and would write to request his services.

"I learned that bears never get up before around 10 in the morning. And you won't see them after one in the afternoon until dusk either. I studied wolves for about two years because I came across a wolf den. This was around 1950. It had been dug out under an eight-foot tree, dead but still standing, on the side of a small lake. All the other dens I have found since have also been near water."

"What a masterpiece that den was. Imagine one long tunnel leading into it that was the entrance, then another one leading away in the opposite direction that was used as an exit. They would have had to pack all the dirt out to carve out both tunnels! That's a lot of work, just to create a safe place away from everyone, a large den that was well under the ground. Because it was wide enough for a man to enter, maybe about two feet in diameter, I was able to crawl into it using a piece of wood with pitch smeared on it so that I could light it and have a full view of the den once I got inside. It looked like it had been used for years. It was a good hideout for them, because Fish and Wildlife used a lot of poison on wolves around this time and it looked like they were able to stay down there for long periods of time."

"Here I had the chance to study a pup's habits. I lit up my pitch torch and crawled inside, so I could see it was about 12 feet around. I put a pup in my backpack and backed out to hear a group of howling wolves, and I realized it was not such a good idea. Otherwise they were quite timid. I learned so much from them! That pup grew up and was just like a dog, would ride inside my pickup. I would go near a wolf area and tie him up and walk out of his sight. Soon all the wolves would come to him and I could count them. They were the most interesting creatures I ever met, very friendly to each other. When they killed a deer, they all fed around it together, no fighting. You could tell they had a lot of feeling for each other. I am not at ease with most people like I was with them. That wolf taught me a lot, and I was grateful to have known him for so long."

"I remember that things were cheap in the fifties, and people were more relaxed, less worried. Once four people came from Georgia, including the editor of *Outdoor Life* and Cropford, the guy who invented the tranquilizer gun, and one airline pilot who flew mail beacon by beacon. What I mean by that is that pilots back then had no navigation equipment like they do today, so they just flew using the beacons as guideposts to see by. There was one family from California that came regularly until the man died in the mid-sixties. And then for two seasons, I had a guiding partner named Walter Ernst. He was a very social Austrian who got people from fishing clubs, mostly rich Germans, to come to the estuaries for trout fishing. We leased part of a guiding area in Atlen from the Tetlan Indians, in northern BC, a tribe that came from the Dees Lake area, good people. It was easy work, fishing from the side of a boat, but it was boring compared to hunting with the hounds. I had to leave the hounds with my sister Anne, and that bothered me."

With Ernst, Percy went to a place in the Queen Charlottes, five miles south of Sandspit, for two seasons, where they built two panabodes. "There are no cougar in the Queen Charlottes. And I missed working with the dogs. One day I took two Germans to fish off a small island there. When we got off the plane, an eagle was trying to get off the water. It did take off, but had to drop the huge fish it was carrying. I ran over and picked it up and said 'Thank you!' Those guys sure were impressed with how easy it was to bring in big fish in the Charlottes."

He came home in the fall of 1971. Someone at Fish & Wildlife told him about a girl named Penny who was going to study cougar three-month-old kittens at Nanaimo Lakes, trying to tame them. She had been given a rifle and was trying to find deer to feed her cubs, but experts had told her that deer came down the valley into the snow, and she found the valleys were mostly logged-off slash areas with no shelter for deer. Percy sought out Penny Brown on New Year's Eve and told her she was wasting her time with the cougar pups, but he helped her with some local deer up in the high timber on the mountain slopes. 'Get them before their eyes are open,' he told her. 'Forget what Fish and Wildlife says.'

But he saw a new opportunity too, and began courting Penny. What they had in common was that they were united by their concern for the pups. For years he'd been looking for a partner to do a cougar study, and Penny had a degree in marine biology. "I couldn't afford to hire her, or any other biologist for that matter, so I married her," laughs Percy. He makes light of the fact that this marriage did not last long either. Again he states his belief that marriage is not for some. "Some people are not the marrying kind. Like you too maybe. We're best left alone." I laugh obligingly. "Does this make us misanthropes? I ask, and he wants me to explain what the word means. "Guess so," he shrugs.

I listen to all the audiotapes Penny made of the study, where she record-ed every minute movement of the cougars, every encounter with cougar faeces. Painstakingly observing details, Penny's voice records them, while listening to Percy dictating what to look for. I look over her log books, her articles in various journals. I try to imagine what she is like. I write her a letter, and she responds by saying only that I am looking for trouble in trying to understand what makes Percy tick. The tone of her letter is a warning: "Don't get on the boat if you don't know how to navigate," she writes.

> *Why don't you talk to me? We are of the same element. Of the same order, and belong together. And whoever wants to expel the other, only expels himself. Do not take comfort in the illusion of an afterlife or another world beyond. Here is where we will battle out our egos. The coldest, the least that we can do – the enormous pain, the enormous loss, the impossibility of leaving this existing confusion other than by dying, disengaging, severing, isolating, only makes death possible.*

Percy admits that he had come to a crossroads in his life when he met Penny. "I had come to a time when I just could not kill cougars anymore. The main thing I wanted to prove by the study was that cougars are not territorial, and that it was the female who seeks out the male scent, not her that leaves the scratch-ings. This is what Percy Sutton always believed too. The reason the female can have kittens any time of year, unlike other carnivores, is that she comes into estrus more than once a year, but if she doesn't mate during estrus, she comes into heat again. Usually cougars give birth every two years or so, and the gestation period is about ninety-six days."

"Fish and Wildlife was not at all helpful in my study. I had asked them to close off an area of 400 square miles to hunting, but all the hunters complained. And they were hard to work with. They seemed to wish I would just go away. So the study got started without them. If I had been hanging by my balls with piano wire waiting on them to help, it would have been uncomfortable for a while. Maybe that would have been fair treatment for some of the top brass at Fish and Wildlife!"

"Before dart guns were invented, I had caught several cougars by roping them. After the hounds put the cat up the tree, I fixed a pulley lower down on the trunk, passed the rope through it, and then climbed up with climbing irons. I would use a forked stick to noose the cougar, then haul it down to the pulley and put the ear tags on it. I had a tranquilizer gun for 1963, developed by a man named Palmer. Once that cougar was treed, which I did seventy-two times during the study, I shot it with the tranquillizer dart, filled with ketamine hydrachloride that BC Fish and Wildlife provided. I also used climbing irons if the cougar was hard to see before I would shoot a dart at it. Almost all the cougars would try to run away, usually a couple hundred yards or so, but would eventually slump to the ground. It usually took about four minutes before the animal was tranquillized. Sometimes I would have to climb up the tree, tie its rear legs, and lower it to the ground."

"Then I attached collars I made myself with two-inch wide elastic material, and the transmitters were put together from purchased parts. Each cougar was given a different channel so I could study twelve to fifteen of them at a time.

Telemetry was just coming in then. Now, telemetric devices are small, weigh less than half a gram, and can even be linked by satellite. But back then, nobody was doing what I was trying to accomplish. Jack Cropford tried to capture a couple of cougar previously but killed them accidentally. I caught a cougar in a tree, which takes ages, drove all the way into town to find a phone since Fish and Wildlife had promised a radio collar if I could tree this cougar. But no one would come and help. They just said, 'It's so and so's day off.' When I went into office and offered to buy the collar that they had originally purchased for deer or elk but hadn't ever used, they gave it to me, but the battery was dead from disuse. Nothing ever worked with them guys."

But Percy's bitterness is tempered by the evenness of his voice. He learned so much from the study, he says, that it was worth any frustration. "Those animals always behaved far better than any human beings I knew during that time."

"While the cougar was knocked out for two and a half hours, I weighed and measured it and checked it over, looking for problems. The average weight of the cougars during the study was anywhere from 100 to 165 pounds, and they were usually about seven feet from nose to tail. We never found any ticks or fleas, not even any broken teeth. One old cougar had his teeth pretty well gone, so some other cougar must have been leaving deer kills behind to feed it. Once the cougars were walking again, I could track them on foot or in my pickup, but we always stayed at least half a mile behind them so we wouldn't frighten them. Or, once a week, we could track them in a plane belonging to this guy I knew in the Qualicum Flying Club. Whenever they stayed in one spot long enough, that was the sign of a kill and I could get there to study them more closely."

"The head of Fish and Wildlife was afraid of being exposed for the poor way he had managed island cougar population once we showed him the facts. Ian Smith, the biologist, was helpful to me."

Percy's first report to Fish and Wildlife was made at the end of the first year of his study. As a result, a bag limit was placed on cougars, and a fixed season for cougar hunting was established. That bag limit is still in place, which makes Percy feel proud. "The top guy at Fish and Wildlife never gave in, sat in his office like a bloody owl. Eventually he killed himself. He was separated from his wife, and needed to show his girlfriend something, I guess." Another Victoria biologist remained unhelpful, although Percy had helped him when he first began his career as a biologist. He also worked with the three top people in the field, yet none would help him finance his proposed cougar study. Finally Percy went to his MLA, but got no help there either. When Percy did a slide show in Parksville, MLA Bob Skelly saw him and arranged an appointment with the Minster of Conservation & Recreation in Victoria. Percy invested $40,000 of his own funds to do the study. He chose to focus on the Northwest Bay logging area. "I knew it would be easy because I had trained my dogs so well."

The politicians in office shifted jobs. Once again Percy tried to get funding, but to no avail. The biologist who succeeded the head of Fish and Wildlife promised Percy $1,500 but did not deliver it to him. Percy says that perhaps the man believed that Percy would abscond with the money. Percy left the office, feeling more determined than ever to complete the study, even if he and Penny were forced to do it by without any financial support. He went back to his mountaintop to think of what to do. He had given himself an interesting challenge, and in his stubborn fashion, was unwilling to give up.

"I sold some property to finance most of the study. In that four-hundred-square mile area, there were 25 resident cougars. The largest cougar we caught was 165 pounds, but usually the males were 125 to 160 pounds, and the females from 85 to 120. I figure most cougars live to be about twelve to fifteen years. The gestation period is about 95 days. The females have young about every two years and raise them alone. In fact, one thing that mystified me was that sometimes the male even kills and eats the pups if the female is out of sight, even covering the carcass with dirt so sun and birds can't get at it. Once a female tried to protect the young one, and fought the male; there were piles of hair and drag marks in the dirt. I still don't know why that is, that males would be so vicious toward their own offspring."

"Nor do we know why cougars scream. It is not to attract the males, because the females do it when no males are present. When the males are moving, they make marks in broken-down wood or loose material, scratch marks, by balancing on the front paws and pushing out with the rear paws. These marks are around one or two inches deep, and eight to ten inches wide. Then they spray on it, so the female can follow the male when she is in season. But I guess I already taught you that."

Percy and Penny moved into the woods and lived with the cougars for five years, completing the study in six. Their shelter was constructed of poles and canvass for the first three years, and then MacMillan Bloedel gave them a place to live and a grant of $10,000. Percy constructed a 30-foot pole with an antenna on top so that they could radio track a large area from the camp; each collar had a different frequency. They treed 72 cougars over six years, a feat Percy attributes to his having good hounds. Every morning they had to make the rounds to check where each cougar was. They rose every day at dawn, carrying heavy back packs, and chased behind the hounds to put the cougars up trees, scurrying over rock faces, rivers and running through canyons. When they could not hear all the cougars by radio, it meant that one of the batteries on the radio collars had died, so Percy would have to tree the cougar again and replace the transmitter. Most of the cougar hunts were very long, lasting eight to ten hours, depending on how old the scent was when the dogs found it. On other fortunate occasions, the cougar could be treed by Penny and Percy within an hour. If a cougar climbed too high, Percy could not fire a dart, or the animal might fall and kill itself.

Once treed, the hounds were tied up to prevent them from attacking a fallen cougar. Percy would take the Cap Chur pistol, drug bottle, syringe, weigh scales, and a radio collar, when Penny produced a camera, notebook, and heavy climbing irons. Using 1 cc of the drug per estimated twenty pounds of the cougar's weight, Percy filled the dart and loaded the pistol, climbed the tree with the irons, and fired the pistol into the animal's haunches. Within 20 seconds, the anaesthetized cougar would usually jump from the tree, run a few hundred yards, then drop unconscious. But if it stayed in the tree, Percy had to climb up, rope its legs, and lower it carefully to the ground. There remained about 15 minutes in which to record the age, condition, and sex of the animal, and to attach the ear tags and radio transmitter collar before it regained consciousness.

From his description of this process, I understand why Percy is in such good shape, and why he can move so swiftly in the bush, as surefooted as a cat. I am certain he could outrun me, even though he is twice my age. Do close observers of wildlife become wild themselves?

"Penny said that in the first 6 months with me on the study she learned more than in all her years at university. Many of the educated people, some with degrees in Biology, who come to work with me even now have no experience in the woods, couldn't show me any evidence of an animal's presence in the woods. I showed them cougar scratches, where bears bit alder trees, how to sense the other occupants of the woods who had been there before them. How to look at the feces and see the dried-up chalky parts where a cougar has ingested the bones of its prey and passed it through a digestive system that is short and efficient. A family of cougars can devour a deer overnight, eating everything but the teeth, hooves, and hide. Waste nothing."

"Fish and Wildlife made a deal with a college in Ohio that we would take students on for a few weeks at a time. We were given $35,000 from the government just to feed them so they could study local wildlife, while the study cost me $40,000 of my own money. Those students were not much use around the camp. The study lasted five years, then I caught the cougars that still had collars on and took them off.

"Fish and Wildlife is embarrassed by the way they have handled wildlife on Vancouver Island. They manage hunters, not wildlife. As if you shoot one animal, just so you can shoot more. Poison the wolves, or trap them as they do nowadays, just so you can hunt deer. They should let the wolves go free, and reduce the bag limit on deer. They tried having no limit on hunting on a 'nonconsumptive basis' both here and in the US, but there were no takers. Even the *Hound* magazine claimed that hounds are not interested in hunting cougars if they can't chew on them after treeing them, which is just untrue. Our study was very successful, more detailed than any that were discussed at the Cat conferences in Nevada and Oregon."

I have been walking in the woods with Percy and I have learned to accept silence, find talking an intrusion. Use my eyes, not my mouth. See scratchings in the dirt that tell wonderful stories. Never feel alone, even with all that quiet around. Learn what he has learned: the art of self-reliance, self-control, and self-improvement. And at home, how to reinvent the domestic. There is a voice below the silence that might be audible after many lives of listening.

"There were two major findings in our study: first, that cougars are NOT territorial. Once I found 13 cougar living in one square mile. They get along as long as there is enough food to go around, just like us. And 80 per cent of the deer killed during the study were in poor condition. Second, that they could be protected if farmers kept Akbash hounds to protect livestock, an idea that Fish and Wildlife refused to support. Akbash treed bears and cougars – not when they were out hunting, just at home protecting my livestock. I never lost any animals. But the government isn't interested in that way of thinking. Just like they could stop killing wolves but aren't interested. Wolves would keep deer population down. In the early 50s, they fed poisoned meat to wolves, and they still trap them. They don't manage animal populations, just manage the hunting, because they don't want protest from the public. I wanted to do the next phase of the study in Strathcona Park, which is why I moved there. Again, I got lots of talk from Fish and Wildlife, but no support. Yet salaried biologists do studies of elk all the time. Still they were happy to give out my unlisted radiophone number if there was a cougar problem they did not want to deal with."

Percy and Penny wrote an article for *The Reader's Digest* called "A Love Affair with the Cougar". It is an apt title. Percy was in love with cougars, all right. But something did not feel right. Percy's intense focus and discipline is finally what allowed him to switch from hunting cougars to preserving them. A change of heart so radical that it could only come from that kind of focus, that kind of love. A transformation that occurs at the border between states of mind.

A change of heart. A flip over to the other side. How does it happen? At what moment do we sense that our lives are moving in reverse? That we have turned a corner? That everything up to this point has been nothing but preparation, wrong-headedness, and dissatisfaction? In the beat of a heart, everything changes. The hunter becomes the hunted, the prey the victor. Once vision clears.

A predator could give you a look that unmans you. And whether it is pelts or information you are after, the hunt remains.

The cougar bounty ended in 1958. The same year I was born. I am exactly half Percy's age.

"I was glad when public pressure put an end to the cougar bounty in 1958. It gave me more places to go without seeing other people. I kept telling them that killing cougars was no longer necessary; I even printed that in the 60s. Six years of study in the Northwest Bay area proved that the population remained the same. And the hunters were badly trained, could only sight one from snow tracks. Hunting or predator control programs are ineffective because removing cougar can only increase density. Transient cougars end up confused and in areas where there isn't enough natural prey. So they attack humans. Finally people began to get more interested in shooting photos than shooting live cougars. I only liked to tree cougars. Some hunters would tell you that the dogs wouldn't tree cougars unless they could chase carcass for a while afterwards. But I hunted with dogs for six years who would rather trail than eat. I didn't kill one cougar during the study. Anyway, it's the chase that is the most important."

"I sure got some nasty letters to the editor about that study. A war of words. Some from people who made their living from killing cougars, but overnight went from cat killer to cat lover. Some wanted me to stop collaring them. A guy from Duncan in particular, who accused me of living on welfare. And then there was always your typical hunter, the big mean hunter in the black and red plaid jacket, hairy-chested, with a size 48-inch chest, and a size one hat, the kind who wanted to get me for trying to close hunting down. Fish and Wildlife had issued notices to leave any cougars with radio transmitter collars alone or return them. But one night in a bar, a local farmer bragged about killing one of these cougars and burning the radio transmitter collar, so Fish and Wildlife sent a goon to nab that farmer and bring him to court, I was subpoenaed, and the judge said how much does this kind of collar cost you? I said $100, so he was fined that amount but Fish and Wildlife kept the money instead of giving it back to me. And that same fellow slandered me in a letter to the editor of the newspaper, and later again in his own book. Too cowardly to do his own study, he had to attack me for mine."

"Then another time a cougar had been shot and turned in. I got a letter from the technician that said contact him by phone to pick up the cougar I had tagged at my expense. I drove all the way from Strathcona to Campbell River to phone, only to be told this guy was on holidays. Nobody respected my study enough to keep me informed about the animals."

"I wanted to continue doing more studies, maybe on another part of the island, but instead I got sidetracked and started building this house in Strathcona

Park. I'll tell you later how that came to pass. But you should know that I ended up working on building this place because everything just fell into place as if it was part of the big plan of what I was to do next with my life. In 1976, when I moved here, there was nothing on the site, and I did not start building until 1981. I bought the site from Wallace Bakkie, the father of the present manager of Strathcona Lodge, Merna Boulding. I had met him on my last day of logging, and found out he had a sawmill in Campbell River called Raven Lumber. I was running a machine that I drove from Nanaimo at fifteen miles an hour, then put it on a barge in Campbell River. Since my main purpose in buying it was to do the study, I was lucky the find out that he was the owner and liked the idea, having no other use for the property."

"When I finished the study, I started gathering material for building since I was planning to go to Strathcona Park area to do a study there, but the Parks people were against it. I was at the Lodge for a few days when one sunny morning, Wallace Baikie said 'Would you like to go for a walk?' So we walked to the ridge above the Lodge. As we came to the top, two deer were feeding on the large, flat ridge, looking almost tame. 'What a nice place!' I said to Wallace. 'I own some acreage here. I would like to sell, but I am stuck with it. Who would want to live all the way up here?' 'I would!' I said. 'So how much do you want?' And we made a deal right there in front of the deer."

"I remember my first view of it, seeing the rock bluff with two duck deer walking across. God, what a beautiful site, I thought! That's when he told me he owned it. When you want to build a place, you know when you've found the right spot. It just feels right. And I knew I wanted to be far from people. The only access was through the lodge, and I had always gotten along with the lodge family."

"I was 62 when I started building. I bought a bunch of windows out of a schoolhouse that was being tore down. I hauled a lot of glass here, and never broke any. And I had lots of stuff I'd scavenged. Guess I have always been a pack rat. That's why I like a large house. You never know when you are going to need something. I actually drew up the plans twenty years ago. The house was built on a large rock bluff. I had to put a footing down around the perimeter, and mix the cement by hand as there was no power and I did not have a mixer anyway. Then I built a two-foot stonewall that was also 2 feet wide.

It took me a whole year to do that, gathering rocks every time I went to town and hauling them back up with me.

"That first winter was rough because the snow was very deep and it was hard to get up there with my truck."

"Later I cut 12x2 planks with a chainsaw to go on top of the stone wall, where the rock bluff ended. These were dry cedar logs, some of which were hard to get to the road, then to the building site, all by hand. Some of them took three days to get up the road to the site. I made all the cedar shakes by hand too, about 19 thousand of them."

"I was able to make the living room 24 feet lower and the greenhouse, down at ground level, was 16 by 40 feet and gave heat to the house. This meant I had warm floors so I wouldn't need to build a fire very often. The frame I built with upright logs on the corners and long logs on top of these, and the ridge poles five feet higher so as to have a slope on the roof; some of these were up to two feet in diameter and 30 feet long.

After cutting his own boards, Percy designed his own crane to hoist large logs that he was using as the center beams of his house; the twenty-foot pole at the side swings around like a boom from the centre pole of about 80 feet and is attached about fifteen feet from the top of the pole by cables he found at an old logging site.

"I used the cables to stake the pole into the ground, by shackling the cables to old tree stumps. After you wind the cable around the stump three times, you put two railroad spikes in to hold the cable to each side of the stump. Then I used three guy wire cables to hold the boom rigid. From the end of the boom, I strung a pulley by using light cable to go to a block of cedar hanging from a guy wire. This allowed you to pull the boom over, and the weight would allow you to swing the boom around when you wanted to bring a log toward the house. At the end of the pulley, I had tongs attached to lift the actual log. I made a turfer, or hand wynch, by myself. This could also be used to swing the shakes up to the roof. I learned the basics in logging camps so that I could rig a spar tree, put the big logs in place with the large come along. Doing this by hand and alone meant a lot of trips back and forth from the log to the come along until it was in place."

The life that Percy chose to make for himself is not in accordance with what could be described as civilized, although it was considered such earlier in the last century. It offers none of the suburban comforts many of us have grown accustomed to. He has built all his houses by himself, and prefers roughly-built housing that provides a simple lifestyle, closely tied to nature. Recently, Percy had to move away from Strathcona, but he says he still misses the place. It was at this house that I came to know Percy and to watch him in action. There is no electricity in the house he built on thirty-seven acres at Strathcona, and he ingeniously built a stone cavern to refrigerate perishable items; above it is suspended a bucket of water with which he can keep the cavern moist and cool.

There were goats and chickens. Percy rose at daybreak every morning and headed to the barn with the dogs and cats to feed them, reminding me that one of the first things he learned from his father was that you always feed the animals before yourself. The Akbash hounds he kept there guaranteed that no hawk took his chickens, and that neither cougar nor bear took his goats. "They treed 26 bears and 14 cougars in the eighteen years I lived there," he says proudly. His tone was more than confident when he described his developments around the property, only 4 acres of which are cleared. He was always a good worker, a homebody whose ability to focus his attention has served him well, he says.

"I decided to leave something of myself here on this island. We live in the best part of the world; I've never been anywhere else except the Yukon and Alaska. I've never been much of a traveler, but I know this whole island like the back of my hand. You have to have some loyalty to what's at home before you can understand the world. There's too much to learn here. I think that's why I was a success with the hounds -- because I could stay focussed on what was in front of me. Most people don't have that kind of discipline anymore. And it makes me proud to live in this place, knowing that I hauled in every log that was used to build it."

"Coming to the barn each morning, the two Akbash hounds and the two border collies and two cats used to follow me, and again in the evening, to milk the goats. I had containers on the floor for each one, and the animals would sit by them as I poured milk into them. It gave me a great feeling of peace, because they never disagreed. When I was done, I would reward them by going to the chicken house and giving them each an egg." He worked continuously during daylight hours, happiest when he had a project to complete. Physical labour obviously gives him great pleasure. "This is a dull life for some people", confesses Percy. "I should have been born twins; I always have so much I want to do and I never get bored. I've never been interested in making money, but I've always had more than I needed."

Grateful for his good health, he attributes this to not having eaten much meat in his lifetime, except for wild game while in the woods to compensate for the unavailability of vegetables during some years, or from the animals whose grazing kept his land cleared. He has always been careful to eat healthy foods. While working on the house when I visited, he usually stopped only to pick a few vegetables from his greenhouse for lunch. Percy is surprised to find he is so capable and healthy at an old age; he expected to slow down physically. He claims he cannot run as fast as he used to, but he says it is a myth that old people lose any of their other abilities.

> *I am solitary. I rely for survival on my individual physical well-being, my strength of mind and character and body. Not the communal hunting skills of a pack. I prefer mutual avoidance, self-regulation of our numbers.*

"This may be hard for you to hear," Percy begins one day. "It's not the style anymore to enjoy work. We loved work, felt really satisfied when we did a good job at something. But today people want to be entertained. They just try to finish work as quick as possible so they can get home to their televisions and lie around, and if they're not careful, they will be entertained to death. Work is something everyone nowadays likes to complain about; you live for your leisure time. Work is something to get through in order to get pleasure; work is not pleasure anymore. Young people are not working alongside their parents and learning the kinds of skills I learned as a child. Few people have any survival skills, and may not know how to live in the woods if faced with another Depression. And believe me, it might not be long until we need those skills again, the way the economy is going. And global warming is changing everything too, especially for the animals I see in the woods today."

Building the house occupied Percy through most of his 60s and 70s. He was proud upon the completion of the main room in particular, which afforded a spectacular view and a dramatic ceiling.

"I came here to Strathcona in 1976. Mac and Blo were very fair with me, so I had the right to gather cedar for shakes. Soon I had a lot of shakes made up. On July 1, 1978, I moved into the new place. I had precut a 10' by 16' cabin with cedar poles, so I had it up and it was liveable in one week. That is where I stayed most of the time while I was building the house.

"There is sure a lot to do on a new place, with no machinery available. I had drawn up a plan some time ago, so I put the lines around and started on the footing, then the foundation, which I did with stones. That took a very long time. I bought a 1974 flat deck truck to move all the shake cedar I'd gathered. It was a very useful truck. I made a winch on the deck so I could load logs and it worked well. I decided to build a chicken house with the same plan, so that way I could correct any faults before the house was built. The chicken house had a central area with three wings going off of it, a total of 1500 square feet, so it was quite convenient to work in it. The overall plan was to have some chickens and goats and two livestock guard dogs."

"There was an article in a goat magazine about a lady in California who was selling some Alpine goats she had brought in from France. She's sold some to some people in Washington who were going to start up a dairy and it didn't work out, so I was able to get four goats from there. Now I started building the goat barn. I'd built barns before, so I could draw up a plan quickly, and I made it 22' by 32' with a loft and a shake roof."

At Strathcona, where I first met him, Percy was constantly busy with building projects, completing the house, gardening, raising animals, tracking cougar in the bush. He still finds pleasure in work well done. This was the eleventh house he has built, and he says he has learned something from each project. "I am an environmentalist, so I don't waste time cleaning the house. I wouldn't think about going outside without wiping my feet!" He gets restless about sitting still for any length of time. Before winter arrived, he packed in a lot of supplies from the road below after going in to Campbell River, so he had to leave his home as little as possible in winter. "I am glad to get home from town, although I know a lot of people at the Co-op now. I met a man I logged with forty years ago. Then I talked with the cashier, who was the daughter of an old friend. Still, all those people make me antsy to get back."

"I am always hauling stuff. I get a lot accomplished. I never waste energy, and I plan to carry something on my way out the door, and to return with something. Each trip should be made efficiently; never go empty-handed. No wasted movement." Percy had a set routine. Every morning, after rising at daylight, he fed his four dogs and cats, then headed to the barn to get the goat's milk for his breakfast, as well as gathering eggs, before heading out for a walk or run for several miles at the back of his acreage. He ate porridge while planning his day. In the fall, getting wood was important, so he spent a couple of hours chopping woodfall. On rainy days, he worked indoors or cleaned out a barn. He was very proud of his enormous garden, fed by the chicken manure compost that he kept in a bin beside the chicken house. Beside it stood an enormous barrel of rainwater, and Percy revealed to me the secret of how he kept it potable: since stagnant water can attract disease-carrying mosquitoes, he always kept a frog in the barrel.

A larger cistern for collecting rainwater towered above the house, and Percy said that a frog or two also inhabited its dark recesses.

Lunch consisted of whatever vegetables he could grab from his greenhouse. Percy always worked until dark, and didn't eat until then so that he wasted no daylight. There is only time to read in the winter months; he has always preferred books about wildlife, or BC history. Often he loses track of time, he says, although he tries to listen to the radio in the morning and at bedtime.

He built a 10x16 foot cabin, a storage building, and then a goat barn (the goats are guarded and herded by the border collies he owns now).

While I stayed with Percy, he taught me how to kill a chicken by holding its artery against the woodblock so that it did not spurt blood. Then he demonstrated how to slit the skin and pull it back so that I wouldn't have to pluck the feathers. "Nobody needs to eat all that fat anyway," he said as he pulled the skin away. There is plenty of wood in store for the big woodstove. A natural teacher, Percy believes in giving me lessons every day that I stay with him. "And most important, always finish what you start." I think about this in the context of writing his life story, and realize that, though it will take me many years, there is an unspoken agreement that I will complete the task he has given me.

Percy designed the house so that hot water pipes run below the greenhouse and provide warmth in the winter; he grew fruit year round, even melon in midwinter. Out on his daily hikes or from the huge picture windows in the house perched above Buttle Lake, Percy watched wolf, bear, and cougar play, telling me that he still continued to learn about wildlife. One of his last concerns was completing the fence around the property entrance from the road, as he was afraid of someone arriving and being bitten by the dogs. "Putting up the fence this summer was a real challenge, all those fence posts, finding old cedar that had been laying around, and sticking to it, even if it's very hard, that's what makes me feel good." Keeping strangers out.

Percy says he never gets lonely. Once or twice a year, he hosts a large party, inviting people up from Strathcona Lodge, many of whom are participants in the Canadian Outdoor Leaders Training (COLT) program. He enjoys the energy of young people, many of whom see him as an elder to turn to when in need of advice. "I've been fortunate to always have a few dollars, and I can't think of a better thing to do than have a big party once in a while. The best one was after my divorce, and that was a very big party. But I don't have much interest in parties any more, it seems. I spent a lot of time alone when I was young, and I guess I am accustomed to that most of the time."

To describe Percy as resourceful is an understatement: he has built a goat house, a chicken house, a horse barn, and a huge house, most of it from salvaged lumber and logging debris. He likes the older generation of people he knows at

Elderhostel for the same reason: the Depression made most of them self-reliant, and they share similar values, believing it better to grow a garden, as they were taught as children, than to buy groceries at the store. What do old people in condos do with their time? he wonders. No weekend conservationist, he takes his commitment to subsistence seriously and he's principled. Perhaps this is what I most admire about him. Even if living close to the edge of the fence has cost him a few jobs and a few friends, he has remained true to himself and moiling for gold has never been his aim.

Percy tells me he has the sense that the house in Strathcona, which I watched him develop, is one of the final houses he will build, and that he has "got it right at last". The view is spectacular, and well worth hiking up to see, I discovered after the first night I climbed the 10-kilometre road.

There is no way to approach the house except by this road, either on foot or by four-wheel drive. So Percy has achieved his desire to live "far from the madding crowd." I too am pleased to sleep on this summit, away from the crowded, noisy city. At night, I hear wolverines and wolves howling. I wake up in the morning to watch the dawn while I am overlooking a somber alpine valley. Blue lights up the mountain crests first in a cobalt wash that lingers, in contrast to the surrounding darkness. It creeps up on the day like a cat. Pinnacles of mountains emerge in pink overtones and mix with the blue-green of first light. The pink intensifies until the peaks are backlit and orange shafts streak the eastern skyline. This penumbral glow could pass for dusk in any other part of the world. It makes me move slowly, want to go back to sleep. But the sun soon advances and there are bright snow sculptures from the evening before, and bright green needles wear tiaras of snow crystals. There is an alabaster mantle of snow that covers the contours of the land, dipping here and rising there. Mosses and lichen protrude like small windows. Chickadees and nuthatches and woodpeckers chatter. All the night creatures – moose, hare, bear – have left their calling cards in the snow, and beg me to get up and explore. It would be hard to stay in bed for long here. Percy wakes up early as well, and makes a fire in the woodstove so that I can prepare my morning tea.

There is a small cabin out back that Percy constructed for $17, scavenging most of the material from old buildings. Here is where he slept while he planned his big house. Initially he built a smaller-scale version of the house, which eventually became the chicken house, complete with stained glass windows that he was able to salvage from abandoned houses. Percy says that he did this because he wanted to work out his mistakes first. It is a chicken house, ornate and large enough that I would be content to live there.

I was most impressed with the design of the stairs leading from below the living room to the greenhouse just below Percy's house on the mountain.

At Strathcona, Percy occasionally took Elderhostel groups on hikes, followed by an evening slide show on wildlife. Most of the hikers were women over sixty, and flirtation was not beyond them, nor beyond Percy. He announces proudly that "I usually manage to escape, although it is not always easy!" While living at Strathcona, Percy still did a lot of work around the lodge, and remains a welcome guest at the dining table any time; the manager Merna says she can never repay him for all the work he has done for Strathcona Lodge. Modestly, Percy will say that such welcome is worth more than any money, and feels he is owed nothing. He says that he likes to play the role of Mountain Man when he is there. "I look at the mist hanging around the mountains and tell everyone it means it will rain in two days. They all look at me with wide eyes. Then two days later, when the sun is still shining, they realize I am just a bullshitter."

He will allow me to interview him only for short periods of time before asking me to leave; as a recluse, he does not like to spend much time with people. He still likes to describe what Vancouver Island was like when he was growing up and compare it to present day island life.

"I spent a lot of time in the mountains as a teen. And before then, too, of course. "I walked from Nanaimo to Cowichan Lake, then on to Nitnat Lake. I was surprised when I lay down at that lake to drink from it and find it was salt water. On the way there I saw a cabin that had been built by cutting an eight-foot block from a windfall spruce that was hollow but had 12 inches of wood around the outside, yet still 8 feet acrossed inside. Someone stood it on end and cut a door and a window out of it and put a shake roof on it. There were so many spruce that grew up to 14 feet in diameter."

"I used to pass these commercial fishing rowboats and canoes out on the lake and I decided when I was just a young kid that I would build one. So I made two dugout canoes, working on them after school. We did not have an adze and I couldn't afford one, so I used an old broken car spring, bent it and sharpened it after heating it over the coals, until finally I beat it into the shape of an adze. I whittled the boats out – it took me months! They all told me I was crazy and would never finish, but that just made me more determined to prove all of them wrong. An old Indian showed me how to balance a dugout canoe. As you are whittling it out, you cannot tell whether you have an equal thickness in the wood on both sides, and naturally it will sink if it's heavier on one side than on the other. So he showed me how you tap out little holes all along the sides – I borrowed my Dad's old drill – and then you fill them in with little pegs when you're done. I let all the other kids use those boats after I finished them."

"In them days, Fish and Wildlife gave us the fry to stock the Nanaimo River watershed, so I packed a lot of them in and stocked the three lakes myself. Some of them grew to around twenty pounds. You know, I spent the whole of my sixteenth year back in those hills! It turned out to be a good thing that I packed those trout fry up to the mountain lakes because then I could take people fishing there later, using a small 10-foot boat I built. One time I took these guys out fishing, and the deal was that I was supposed to provide lunch. Well, lunch for me was just whatever vegetables I could grab out of our garden. So I had lots of tomatoes and cucumbers, but the one guy said he didn't like neither. So he sure was hungry by the end of the day! I built two of those kinds of punt boats, and carried them up to the first lake, called Labour Day Lake, in the springtime, dragging first one, and then the other, across the crust of ten-foot snow drifts because there were no roads in those days. It took me two days to get them there. From there the water runs into the small second lake called Indian Lake, and after that into Cameron Lake. It was not easy dragging that boat up steep trails across a crust of early spring snow, and then across the ice. Some timber cruisers saw me doing this and thought I was nuts when I asked how far was it to the fourth Nanaimo Lake. I was just having them on, and they thought I was stupid, so they told me to keep going. As if I didn't know those backwoods better than they did."

"In the mid-20s, when logging was at low elevation, the deer and blue grouse populations increased, as the bush, vines, and berries grew very well. While walking on the logging railway with my Dad, it was possible for us to count up to eighty deer in an hour. This carried on into the 30s, as logging at that time was done by railway. Therefore there was no way that the public could get into the backwoods without walking for miles on the railway, and vast areas had little or no hunting. At the same time, there were fires, many of which were several hundred acres in size; there were no water bombers at that time. So the predator population also increased, and wolves, cougars and bears thrived on the roots, berries and grass."

"By the 40s, most logging was done by the patch method; this involved an area of two thousand feet in each direction which was logged and then an equal-sized area left untouched before repeating the logging patch again. By this method, a firebreak was created since the timber held the moisture quite well. This made for ideal conditions for game, including elk, since the logged area was like a garden in which game could graze. If the snow became too deep, they went into the standing timber, where the temperature was warmer and the snow brought down branches and lichen. There were still vast areas of wilderness, so there was little contact between people and predators."

"I guess the biggest change that happened after that was that logging was done by truck rather than rail. And the railway changed from steam to diesel. I saw only steam locomotives when I first started working in the woods, and mostly we felled trees by handsaw and cut them into lengths by hand as well. The chain saw also came into use. This sped logging up and made it possible to go higher up into the mountains. Higher elevations also resulted in winter layoffs."

"Many more people got hounds at this time; most were loggers who hunted during winter layoff season by driving along the roads and looking for cougar tracks. Cougars were killed in great numbers, as there was still a bounty on cougars. In 1948, there were 725 cougars killed in BC. There were still great numbers of deer in the fifties and the grouse numbered in the thousands. There were elk out everywhere when I walked. At this time, the human population was growing, causing more contact with the predators. It was explosive, all this growth in population. Areas that were logged earlier were growing back, and trees measured twenty to thirty feet in height, forming a canopy, which blocked the sunlight, so the deer had no feed. Since deer hunters had access to most logging roads, many deer were shot from the roads. Because of the high number of predators and the poor feeding conditions for deer, they went down in great numbers, many starving to death, as they were not able to get into the timber when the snow got deep. There was no closed season on hunting, nor was there any bag limit. Clear cuts became much larger than they were before because logging could be done so quickly; this also meant that the wildlife never again reached the numbers that it had before."

"From 1922 to 1954, there were 13, 265 cougars killed and 22,679 wolves. A lot of wolves were poisoned by Fish and Wildlife, who employed ten predator hunters at the time. Every effort was made to wipe out the wolves and the cougar; fortunately, it was not successful. I started a study in 1972, with no help from Fish and Wildlife, and did come up with some answers as to how far cougars traveled, and how many deer they killed. Doing the cougar study for five years with transmitters taught me even more about tracking. If I knew when I was a tracker what I know after that study, I could do a lot better job killing cougars now because I know where to find them."

"Because some of the predators, deprived of deer, killed livestock, I tried to encourage farmers to have livestock guard dogs. I raised a litter of Akbash hounds from two I imported, most of which ended up going to ranches in the north. Farmers around here blunder along in the same way, complaining that their livestock are being killed but are unwilling to protect them. I tried to convert local farmers to the idea of conserving rather than reducing the cougar population, but nobody was too interested. Dogs that run in packs are more of a danger to sheep than wild predators. I learned about Akbash hounds -- famous for protecting livestock from predators -- through reading, so I know that this breed has been used everywhere in the European Pyrenees, and in the Comodores in Turkey. For centuries. In fact, it was originally the same dog in all those areas, but it adapted to individual environments. I brought my first male pup over from Turkey in 1985. Then I got a female from Oregon, raised its pups and sold them to local ranchers. Without any training they both started right off guarding the property and treeing bear and cougars. The male got to be 150 pounds, and I called him Wesum. He would stay on a rock bluff all night, overlooking the whole area. They spent a lot of time with the goatherd, and treated deer much the same as the goats. One morning Wesum came to me and he had a chick between his legs; it had slipped through a hole in the fence and been separated from the chicken. They rescued a blue jay too. And once Wesum came out of the barn, breaking the window, to tree a bear. When they treed a cougar, they would stay at the base of the tree until I got there. Oh, those dogs gave me so much. I know that this is my heaven!"

Percy's fascination with domesticated animals, dogs, has in no way tamed his fascination with wild animals like cougars – he doesn't see any border between them, in fact. Ironically, it was farmers who were enticed in the 1850's and onwards to become cougar hunters, initially out of a desire to protect their livestock. Later, attracted by the bounty money, they became specialized in tracking.

> *But I am the supreme tracker. King of the beasts on this continent. I have confused you for years because I am such an enigmatic combination of secrecy and curiosity, docile as a kitten but savage as a god. I am drawn to you, but you frighten me too. Since you will not let me be, I will take your sheep, your dogs, whatever small offerings you choose to leave unguarded at the foot of the world, the altar that was formerly my playground and my kingdom.*

"Look, Vancouver Island is 13,000 square miles and much of it is no longer suitable for wildlife; the opposite was true when I was growing up. It was often unsuitable for us. We are probably down to 4,000 square miles that are still bush, and it feels like the island I grew up on is getting smaller all the time. People spout all this bullshit about what they'd like to leave as a legacy to their grandchildren. Should it be parkland? What good is it if there is no vegetation, and so no deer or elk? It's only now that people are becoming conscious of animal conservation. I had to laugh at the hippies in the 60s who started this whole emphasis on recycling. We were raised with that attitude -- you didn't waste anything! There is too much money in logging now. When I look at young teenagers driving brand new thirty-thousand dollar vehicles around in Gold River, I realize it is all this affluence that is killing us."

"This new island highway is a good example of unnecessary destruction of wildlife habitat; it wasn't needed at all. I've seen a big difference in the valley here, which, after all, was only mapped 100 years ago. For one thing, the animal population has been decimated. Before, the road ended at Buttle Lake, and you had to hike in. I watch wood chips being hauled to Gold River, which is an inefficient use of trucks. The railroad in the old days made more sense. There is nowhere on the island you cannot reach by car now, and that's a real shame."

"Let nature take its course. The wolf kill program on Vancouver Island is senseless. And what they have done to this park! My God! I have loved this valley since 1950, before they dammed it and made it stump ugly. They are thinking of changing the park into an area where they can log and allow mine exploration. Some things should just not be tampered with. I worry about the wildlife here. This has always been a natural protected area. And people are growing more afraid of predators these days. I am only afraid of men now." He is thoughtful for a moment. I have never heard him use the word "love" before; as a pragmatic Scotsman, it is not in his vocabulary. And his dreams are practical ones. Thoughtful men are dedicated to conservation. Perceptive men can be persuaded into believing in it; but those ardent materialists who form most of our culture may need to be frightened into believing in conservation. The enemy of conservation is the enemy of himself, says Percy.

I listen once more to Percy's tapes of the cougar study. The low, clear whistles of the males. The high-pitched scream of a female. "I would like to start another study. I tried it with a girl biologist for a year, but it was a waste of time." Then Percy repeats one of his favourite adages: "I got calluses on my feet finding out about cougars, while some biologists got them on their behinds."

"I've known the area around here since 1952, whereas most biologists spend almost no time in the woods. I would like to do the same area I covered before; it would be easy. That girl couldn't even tell that there was a difference from cougars here to those down island. Here they travel less, since there's more game available. Just like when I did my study, there were all those longhaired students from Antioch College who came up to see what I was doing; they were sympathetic but still pretty ignorant. We need to do a study of the Strathcona Park area because it should be done in an area where there are few humans most of the year."

One day I meet Percy in Qualicum. He is outside his truck, but does not get into the driver's seat after I have slung my backpack onto the floor of the passenger seat and hopped into the truck. He remains outside the truck for some time. With patience and a shocked expression on his face, he picks up the trash and bottles left behind by a police car that has just pulled away. Nearby is the vomit of the teenager who was arrested. "I don't get it. Why are they out drinking instead of working, and where do they get the money for this? And why don't they clean up after themselves, have some respect for the land?" He holds up an empty bottle of Scotch severed at the neck. "It's the same in the woods. I can hardly see tracks for all the trash and dirt bike tire marks, and all the hydro lines make it hard for me to know where I am walking. The deer know it too, and they are confused."

Sickness reflects a disruption of the harmony and balance among all aspects of this world. Every element in nature has evil and good aspects, but evil is becoming dominant. This is because you do not know how to conduct yourselves. A few months in the woods with me would cure you. But you are stupider than my new cubs were. I wish I knew the medicine to bring these raging forces under control and defeat the sickness. But my mother was killed by a hunter before she finished teaching me that lesson. I am an adolescent seer with precognitive powers that you cannot understand anymore. I pity you, devolved creature. We are aware of each other's presence, but silent. You watch my ears go up and down, the flag posts of peace or aggression. At half-mast, you are uncertain. Flattened, my ears are alert. The wilderness is perilous and unforgiving. Can you enter it? Observe me long enough and you will meet your animal self. Envision me and I will appear.

No moon tonight. A short journey can seem interminable. Don't force the pace. Harness patience to avoid carelessness. Working blind, let your other senses be sharpened.

No long-distance runner, I am wary of being hunted. Your hounds sense this, gave you new noses, and now you tree me. I preferred the Indians' wolf dogs, not all this deep baying and racket. It has made me overly cautious. I have learned of new enemies. I will avoid your kind from now on. Look at me – smaller than my an-

cestors! They never stayed in coniferous forests with squirrels and hares. But, if I am forced to live here, I will become resourceful.

On another day, Percy and I drove to hear a park ranger's presentation on cougars near Ralph River. After it was over, his anger at German tourists being fed lies by "a nobody who knows nothing and just wants to impress people with scary stories" made Percy unusually agitated. His voice was not as slow and as calm as usual.

At seventy-six, Percy fell in love with Ilse Hill, a Danish woman four years older than himself. She had met him through Elderhostel, when Percy was leading seniors on a hike and doing a slide show. For several years, Ilse visited Percy at his home in Strathcona, helping him repair the roof on the goat barn after it caved in under heavy snow.

They built gardens together, and began to spend more time together. Percy complained to me once that this woman kept coming and cleaning up his place so well that he could not find anything anymore. Accustomed to frequent female visitors, he said that this one seemed to be coming around more than the others, and staying for longer periods of time. I could not tell if he was genuinely upset by all this attention, or merely feigning annoyance. And then Percy became very ill one winter at Strathcona, and Ilse decided to take him down from his hill and nurse him back to health at her home on Salt Spring Island. Eventually he realized that he would be unable to continue caring for all his animals in Strathcona, and moved in with Ilse, putting his home on the mountain up for sale. I enjoy teasing Percy about the irony of a diminutive "older woman" knocking him off his pedestal on the top of his mountain in Strathcona. "How the mighty have fallen!" I tell him.

Percy was determined that he would sell only to someone who would steward the land well and genuinely cared for it, rather than merely for profit. He said that what he would miss the most were the splendid views that were afforded him from his deck in Strathcona.

Percy and Ilse have now been together for almost a decade. I visit them frequently on Salt Spring Island, where Percy still leads seniors on hikes, and belongs to the Nature Trail Club. The two of them play golf together several times a week. Ilse helps Percy design petitions and organize local groups to protest what Percy still declares is the unfair persecution of predators. His fighting spirit and his energy remain strong, even though he is in his eighties.

In 2002, Percy began a petition to end the proposed culling of wolves on Vancouver Island, published in local newspapers. A proposal to the Environment Minister by government biologists called for the killing of one hundred and twenty wolves and an undetermined number of cougars over the subsequent three years, in order to increase the deer population. Percy showed me the article in *The Cowichan Valley Leader*, and laughed when he read what the "experts" at Fish and Game stated: that wolves often kill deer that they don't consume, and the cougar and deer eat a deer a week. But when he pointed to all the other errors of fact in the article, he was clearly incensed. And in fact his anger at predator mismanagement provoked him to organize a petition, carefully outlining the facts once more. "It's the same old thing," Percy sighed. "They will just never learn from the past, and cannot seem to get it right."

Percy circulated his report and petition in early September. In the petition, he stated that each cougar kills a deer every ten to twelve days, then fasts for three or four days, making an average of thirty deer killed a year. Cougars reproduce only every two years, he reminded the petitioners, and while there may be up to five in a litter, and usually only two or three survive, as the male will sometimes kill the young. Other females nearby can result in a fight between the adults. The females normally stay in small areas and rarely trouble humans, while the males can travel up to twenty miles a night and therefore could be seen and counted several times a night, resulting in errors in estimates of total cougar populations. He concluded the petition by writing that

Problems, as a rule, are caused by orphaned kittens and young males. The orphaned kittens have missed the training by their mothers on how to survive and they will subsequently kill whatever they can. We are against any program to cull the cougar population. However if such a program to cull the cougar population on Vancouver Island were to be undertaken, then no female cougars should be included in the culling process. As the study done by Percy Dewar indicates, the young cougar stay with, and receive training from, their mothers for up to two years. Without this training, these orphaned cougars have the potential to cause problems.

Working with the Cowichan Valley Naturalists' Society, Percy and other protesters succeeded in postponing the predator culling, and by the end of September, *The Pictorial* reported that "narrowly focused predator culls…remain an ad hoc solution that lack context, and that more concrete research is needed on why deer populations fluctuate." It concluded that, in any case, there was also no recent or accurate inventory of the deer population. Percy was jubilant. As he was able to institute a bag limit on hunting cougars many years ago and to stop the bounty so many years ago, he was now able to triumph once more.

Recently, Percy showed me all the Provincial Game Commission reports he has kept, small blue books recording numbers of hunting and fishing accidents, trout plantings, prosecutions, revenues derived from fur trading licenses, bounties paid out by the government, and the results of animal population surveys. These reports go back to the forties, and are packed with fascinating information. "When my brother Jim died, and he'd been the Predator Control guy for so many years, I kept all the blue books, mostly to satisfy my own curiosity. But also because I knew that the public was being misinformed. And it is useful on an occasion like this to be armed with the facts. And to be able to tell people that in the 1940s, the British Columbia government hired four full-time hunters in order to try to wipe out the cougar population on Vancouver Island, but was forced to cancel the bounty, paying up to forty dollars for each animal killed, because the endeavour failed. It's good to show people how history just repeats itself."

It is clear to see that Percy's sustained enthusiasm for such causes has also inspired Ilse. When they speak together, there is a teasing spark in their eyes that reminds me of teenagers. He credits Ilse with his being alive today, and is grateful that they have one another to sustain themselves through their final years. Both of them suspect that the reappearance of skin rashes that have plagued Percy for 50 years may be associated with Lupus, a condition under which the skin cannot breathe, eventually smothering vital organs like the kidney and the liver. Percy has good days, and he has bad days where he cannot sleep because he is in such pain, and so itchy. But in his usual taciturn fashion, he refuses to complain. He says he misses the quiet on Strathcona, and is disturbed by Ilse's dishwasher. He is ill at ease on the telephone, and prefers face-to-face conversations. He tells me he is golfing regularly and that he is quite good at it. "I know, I know," I interject, "If you can't be good at something, why bother doing it at all?" When he picks me up in his battered pickup, the stoic face that greets me reminds me that this is someone who has been disciplined never to complain, just to endure. He says he still wants to build another place, feels bored when he isn't planning the construction of something. His sense of humour remains, and he makes a joke about the new pair of specialized shoes he has just purchased for $250. "That's more than I spent on my acreage over 40 years ago!"

I will only communicate this to you by the scratch marks in the dirt. Scent markers, which if you curl your lip in a grimace called a flehman, engaging your special olfactory organ on the roof of your mouth, will tell you all you need to know about me. Elusion is a transient survival mechanism. Yet my welfare mirrors your well being, and you still stalk me. Maybe there are questions you want to ask of me. You talk of your fear of my extinction publicly, but privately you send your emissaries for one more trophy. The value in scarcity increases. Soon you will don my mask and take on my spirit, try to become m. You will revere me even more after my slaughter. You will make a ceremony of my death, and only my mask will appear after I am gone. You will string my teeth into necklaces, wrap your male infants in my skin, and nail my head above your hearth.

It is growing warm up here. I pant to lower my body temperature until I can find shade. Come winter I will replace this summer coat with a denser, darker version. I can adjust my skin surface temperature to the ambient temperature and survive extremes of temperature much better than you can. Still, there are no deer left. Ranchers using public land to graze their herds give me easy pickings, raised on my doorstep. But their grazing has reduced the forage, and I am losing my way, my markers, and the elk and the deer have been scared away by a lack of food. Of course when the sheep are gone, I will look for other small prey, crouched over, huddled, fearful. And then the guns will echo along the mountain ranges once more, louder and fiercer this time. At last I will become truly invisible. At last I will triumph over all this.

"Loads of people ask me what we can do to help preserve the cougar population. There are many things, of course, but few people are willing to put them into practice, or to be concerned enough to take a stand. We could learn more from Europeans about managing wildlife. Biologists now have no conviction, they are just afraid of losing their jobs even though they know predators have got to be among other animals. Now predator guard dogs have been very successful. For instance I never lost one chicken, put bears and cougars in trees with my dogs. I believe animals learn to walk around the Strathcona place now rather than through it, which was their habit before. From their snow tracks I could tell that there are around the same number now as there were when I got there. But in other parts of B.C., the number of cougars is dwindling, especially in the Kootenays and the Cariboos. In the Western U.S., they are financing studies -- ones that are far less detailed than mine, I must say -- because they know cougars are becoming extinct. We will soon have fewer of everything, unless conditions improve. I am not hopeful. We are making so much disappear. And soon I will disappear too."

"When I die, I want to be cut up into little pieces and fed to the cougars on Vancouver Island. I hope I die in the bush."

A woman watches television in her home near the forest. There is a program about predator attacks, a call by outraged citizens to renew the bounty against cougars and wolves. She is startled by a sudden noise, thinking she hears a wild animal outside. But it is just the dishwasher, clanking to announce its presence. Nature is at its silent best outside her screen door. She listens intently. There is no response. Maybe this is the final mystery: that creatures can die leaving no mark. Like a good camper who leaves no trace. She closes the sliding glass door. What used to be a reflection is no more. There are no boundaries. And while we are looking through a glass darkly, trying to understand what is on the other side, the glass turns transparent.

Printed in the United States
by Baker & Taylor Publisher Services